BODIES

BIG IDEAS

General editor: Lisa Appignanesi

As the twenty-first century moves through its tumultuous first decade, we need to think about our world afresh. It's time to revisit not only politics, but our passions and preoccupations, and our ways of seeing the world. The Big Ideas series challenges people who think about these subjects to think in public, where soundbites and polemics too often provide sound and fury but little light. These books stir debate and will continue to be important reading for years to come.

Other titles in the series include:

BODIES

Susie Orbach

PROFILE BOOKS

First published in Great Britain in 2009 by
PROFILE BOOKS LTD
3A Exmouth House
Pine Street
London EC1R 0JH
www.profilebooks.com

Some small part of this material originally appeared, in a slightly different form, in Susie Orbach, 'Fashioning the Late Modern Body: The Democratisation of Beauty' in *Cultural Politics in a Global Age*, edited by David Held and Henrietta Moore (Oneworld Publications, Oxford, 2008) and Susie Orbach, 'How can we have a body? Desire and Corporeality', in *Studies in Gender and Sexuality*, Vol. 7 No. 1, 2006, pp. 89–111.

1 3 5 7 9 10 8 6 4 2

Typeset in Minion by MacGuru Ltd
info@macguru.org.uk

Printed and bound in Italy by L.E.G.O. S.p.A., Lavis, (TN)

A CIP catalogue record for this book is available from the British Library.

ISBN 978 1 84668 019 9

FSC
Mixed Sources
Product group from well-managed
forests and other controlled sources
Cert no. SGS-COC-2939
www.fsc.org
© 1996 Forest Stewardship Council

CONTENTS

To Lukas, Lianna, Lilli,
Judah, Lahn and Lila

INTRODUCTION

Every day my inbox, like most people's, fills with invitations to enlarge the size of my penis or my breasts, to purchase the pleasure and potency booster Viagra and to try the latest herbal or pharmaceutical preparation to lose weight. The exhortations have fooled the spam filter and the popular science pages, which too sing of implants and pills to augment body or brain and new methods of reproduction which bypass conventional biology. Meanwhile little girls can go on the Miss Bimbo website to create a virtual doll, keep it 'waif' thin with diet pills and buy it breast implants and facelifts. They are being primed to be teenagers who will dream of new thighs, noses or breasts as they peruse magazines which display page after page of a look that only ten years ago had the power to evoke horror in us as we recoiled at skeletal models reminiscent of famine victims. Simultaneously, government pronouncements grimly warn of an epidemic of obesity. Your body, all these phenomena shout, is your canvas to be fixed, remade and enhanced. Join in. Enjoy. Be part of it.

As a practising psychotherapist and psychoanalyst, I see the impact of calls for bodily transformations, enhancements and 'perfectibility' in the consulting room. People do not necessarily come in with particular body troubles, but whatever their other emotional predicaments and conflicts, concern for the body is nearly always folded into them, as though it were perfectly commonplace to be telling a story in which body dissatisfaction is central. Like many of us, the people I work with wish to and do reshape their bodies in both small and dramatic ways. They find fault with their bodies and say it makes them feel better, more in control, to improve them. Like most of us, they do not like to believe that they are being unduly influenced by outside pressures and may disdain such an idea, with its crude sense of manipulation. Whether followers of fashion or health trends or not, we take for granted that looking good for ourselves will make us feel good. And yet there is a subtle tracery of outside urgings which works on us, creating a new and often dissatisfied relationship with our bodies.

The sense that biology need no longer be destiny is gaining ground and so it follows that where there is a (perceived) body problem, a body solution can be found. A belief in both the perfectible body and the notion that we should relish or at least accede to improving our own body has not, however, solved the problem. On the contrary, it has exaggerated the problem and contributed to what we observe today – a progressively unstable body, a body which to an alarming degree is becoming a site of serious suffering and disorder.

Our bodies are increasingly being experienced as objects to be honed and worked on. Men are targeted with steroids, sexual aids and specific masculine-oriented diet products. Children's bodies, too. Photographers now offer digitally enhanced baby and child photos – correcting smiles, putting in or removing gaps between the teeth, straightening out wobbly knees, turning little girls into facsimiles of china dolls. The web addresses of these conjurors show no sense of irony (see, for example, www.naturalbeauties.homestead.com), since they believe that enhancing photos is a version of natural beauty, the real thing. Girlie-sexy culture now entrances more rather than fewer of us. Putting the body on show and making it appear 'attractive' are presented as fun, desirable and easily accessible. Body beautiful and the goal of perfectibility have been democratised. Invitingly set out as available to everyone in any country whatever their economic situation, the right body is trumpeted as a way of belonging in our world today. This democratic call for beauty, disconcertingly, wears an increasingly homogenised and homogenising form, with the images and names of the global style icons pressed on the lips and the eyes of the young and the not so young. While some people may be able to opt in and do so joyfully, a larger number cannot. For the democratic idea has not extended to aesthetic variation; instead the aesthetic has paradoxically become narrower over the last few decades. The slim aesthetic – with pecs for men and ample breasts for women – bedevils those who don't conform, and even those who do happen to fit can carry a sorrowful insecurity about their own bodies.

A constant fretfulness and vigilance take hold for many from the moment they wake until the time they fall asleep. Their bodies are on high alert. The norm has become to worry. In another time, we would have called such anxieties an illness and, seeing how many suffer, we would have called it an epidemic. But we don't. We have become so implicated in variants of body preoccupation ourselves, and girls and women in particular so colonised by it, that the preoccupation has become second nature – almost 'natural' and invisible.

If, however, we do look, we see that the preoccupation with the body is disturbing in its capacity to affect almost an entire life, from childhood through to old age. Young boys' yearnings to emulate a great sportsman's agility are now focused on the desire for the look of a six-pack. Girls as young as four have been made bodily self-conscious and are striking sexy poses in their mirrors which are more chilling than charming, while greater numbers of women in old age homes are showing signs of long-term eating disorders. Few would say that such concerns come only from outside pressures. We experience the wish for more perfect bodies as our own desire, as indeed it is, yet it is hard to separate out the ways bodies are seen, talked about and written about and the effect of that on our personal perception of our own bodies and other bodies. The body has become a new focus in both women's and men's lives, no longer something secure or ordinary in itself. A new rhetoric of detox, weight training, brushing, irrigation, cleansing is proposed, inclining us to watchfulness and determination where our body is concerned. Those who had previously paid little heed to fashion or health now find themselves caught up in attempts to make the best of themselves and to take responsibility for their health and well-being. The individual is now deemed accountable for his or her body and judged by it. 'Looking after oneself' is a moral value. The body is becoming akin to a worthy personal project.

Feature writers fill endless column inches with advice about how we should care for ourselves. Television programmes focus on the bonuses, the necessity and the moral superiority of paying attention to individual health and beauty. Politicians urge us to take personal responsibility. Meanwhile our visual world is being transformed through an intensification of images which represent the body and parts of the body in ways that artfully convey a sense that our own bodies are seriously in need of reshaping and updating. Without even noticing we may willingly accept the invitation, eager to stay up to date.

The preoccupation with thinness and beauty which has been eroding individual self-worth for years has recently been joined by another fixation: the rising rate of obesity. An ordinary reliance on one's body to signal its dietary needs appears to have evaporated, to be replaced by scrutiny and despair as one struggles to control a body now designated as rapacious. Diet companies are growing, with a newcomer, NutriSystem, hitting the *Fortune* 500 fastest-growing companies as it moved from profits of $1 million in 2004 to $85 million in just two years. New gyms and health bars keep opening. New foods keep being invented. Magazines devoted to weight, shape and health expand their circulation. A relentless desire to reshape the body is evident everywhere. Cosmetic surgical procedures are occupying more of our television screens and our purses (with a growth rate of $1 billion a year), implying that resculpting is easy and an expression of self-worth. On top of all this, reproduction is being reconfigured: young women are freezing embryos for future use, having access to IVF at ever-younger and ever-younger ages, and a new phenomenon, the transgendered man, is reproducing.[1]

Late capitalism has catapulted us out of centuries-old bodily practices which were centred on survival, procreation, the provision of shelter and the satisfaction of hunger. Now, birthing, illness and ageing, while part of the ordinary cycle of life, are also events that can be interrupted or altered by personal endeavour in which one harnesses the medical advances and surgical restructurings on offer. Our body is judged as our individual production. We can fashion it through artifice, through the naturalistic routes of bio-organic products or through a combination of these, but whatever the means, our body is our calling card, vested with showing the results of our hard work and watchfulness or, alternatively, our failure and sloth. Where once the body of the manual worker could be easily identified through brawn and muscle, now it is the middle-class body that must show evidence of being worked on at the gym, through yoga or any number of body practices which aim to display what the individual has achieved through diligent exercise. For young people it is very much a case of take care or beware. Users of social networking sites often post unflattering pictures of individuals which are then 'snarked' and negatively commented on.[2] The rise of public bitching about the body is accompanied by the dissemination of images throughout the World Wide Web.

Commercial pressures delivered today by celebrity culture, branding and industries which make their profits by destabilising the late-modern body have eradicated most of our prior feeling towards and understanding of the body. Our bodies no longer make things. In the West, robotics, mechanised farm equipment, pre-prepared goods from food to building packs, motorised transport, high-tech warfare and so on have replaced much ordinary physical activity and labour. We don't tend to repair things either, for mass production means it is cheaper to replace them. Our relations to the physical and physical work are shifting. Where working-class bodies were shaped by the musculature of heavy physical work; low-paid jobs in the service industry and computer-based jobs across the class spectrum leave no such physical indicators. Indeed, many of us have to make an effort to move about during the day or as we work. In an updating and democratising of the habit of the leisured classes (who didn't do physical labour) of decorating themselves as amusement and social marker, we are invited to take up this activity too. Thus we can observe something new occurring. Our bodies are and have become a form of work. The body is turning from being the means of production to the production itself.

The fallout from these changes is visible in the consulting rooms of psychotherapists, psychologists, counsellors, psychoanalysts and doctors. Here we see a rising number of cases of what I call bodily instability and body shame. It has become ever more evident that our understanding of bodies needs new explanations and theories. Whether we're trying to fathom the willingness and desire of so many people to change the size or shape of their penises, breasts, bums and tums, or attempting to comprehend the experience of a man with a phantom limb, or decoding troubling psychosomatic symptoms, or dealing with anorexia, bulimia and any of the body dysmorphias, the Descartian or Freudian conceptions of the body now seem inadequate. The mind–body link is being transformed. Orthodox psychoanalytic theory about the mind's ability to commandeer the body has fallen short. In this time of body instability what becomes ever clearer is that the natural body is a fiction. A thorough consideration of bodies today is urgently required.

Of course, looking around the world at the many varieties of bodily gesture and decoration,[3] it is easy to see the ways in which bodies have always been an expression of a specific period, geography, sexual, religious and cultural place. Lengthening necks, decorating faces, veiling heads, revealing ankles, wearing business suits, colouring hair, tattooing arms, binding girl's feet, inserting gold teeth, covering heads, practising circumcision on males and females, or painting fingernails in particular ways are all immediate signs of being marked or marking oneself as belonging to a specific group. Bodies are recognised by the costumes and the gaits that befit the groups we come from and wish to belong to or identify with. Our bodily codes and behaviours constitute who we are. And while we might not regard them as purposeful practices, they nevertheless show us that our taken-for-granted body is neither natural nor pure but a body that is inscribed and formed by the accretion of myriad small specific cultural practices. It is now possible to see that, in certain respects, there has never been an altogether simple, 'natural' body. There has only been a body that is shaped by its social and cultural designation. What I shall argue in this book, however, is that current cultural discourse on the body means that we have entered a new epoch of body destabilisation, and that there is a new franticness surrounding the body induced by social forces which are absorbed and transmitted in the family, where we first acquire our bodily sense.

This does not mean that we experience our bodily practices as alien. As we perform our exercises, do our hair, put on our clothes, we are underpinning how we wish to be seen and how we see ourselves. We prepare with pleasure. Our bodily practices don't come to us from on high as a prescription to follow like some catechism. Cultural identities are transmitted in the most ordinary and primary of interactions between babies and parents. They are the very stuff of the relationship. The way babies are carried, nurtured, spoken to, fondled, fed and engaged with represents not only a set of cultural practices that mothers, fathers, nannies, grandparents have absorbed and are passing on; they also become the essence of the child's experience of his or her own body.

It was ever thus and was not something we needed to pay much heed to. Boy children raised to be warriors developed the necessary physical and emotional attributes that entailed, while girls were raised to be demure and sit quietly and sweetly with their legs crossed. Their bodies were appropriately expressive without being questioned. An English schoolboy of the 1960s would be instantly recognisable and distinguishable from his German or Chinese counterpart, by his posture, his clothing and the physical field his body occupied. Each boy's embodiment was constitutive of his sense of self. Bodies are first formed in infancy and shaped according to the social and individual customs of the families they are born into, so that they reflect the kinds of bodies that are suited for the lives they will need to live.

Of course, sometimes bodies went wrong. Not medically or organically, but they somehow refused to behave as they were meant to. They stopped working quite right. A limb became paralysed, or a woman appeared with a swollen pregnant-looking stomach when neither intercourse nor impregnation had taken place. A man might become sexually obsessed with a high heel and be unable to ejaculate without fondling or seeing one. Such phenomena captivated Sigmund Freud in the late nineteenth century and he became fascinated by the relationship between mind and body: more specifically, the routes of the troubled body in the workings on the mind. Talking to his patients, he set about tracing the origins of bodily symptoms for which there was no medical basis in the individual's physical make-up or heredity. From there he drew links between what individuals had experienced, their construction and memory of what had happened and how they made sense of that experience in the light of their unconscious longings and conflicts. Freud convincingly demonstrated that the mind could exert a powerful influence on the body. His work, although slow to be taken up initially, has revolutionised how we see the relationship and the interaction between the mind and the body.

Freud's insights have deservedly compelled us for over a hundred years. They are not only the basis of a psychoanalyst's stance and toolkit but have penetrated the medical field so that it is now commonplace to try to evaluate the impact of stress on the immune, endocrine and digestive systems or on the largest of our organs, the skin. Today we don't think twice about linking eczema with psychological distress. We don't dismiss the chemical irritants that provoke itching and redness but we rarely stop there; we pursue the relationship between emotions, personal story and the various body systems.

What Freud showed us, first of all, was that a 'natural' human sexuality was a misperception. Sexual desire is replete with conflict, longing and fantasy. In our epoch, I contend, the body itself has grown as complicated a place as sexuality was for Freud's. It too is shaped and misshaped by our earliest encounters with parents and carers, who also contain in themselves the forces and imperatives of our culture, with its panoply of injunctions about how the body should appear and be attended to. Their sense of their own bodily lacks and strengths, their hopes and fears about physicality, will play themselves out on the child. In my consulting room, their impact on the child's bodily sense and his or her adult wearer's bodily instability becomes clear. What I am finding new and troubling is the prevalence of distressed parental bodies inside the body experience of the adults I see. What is emerging now is a transgenerational transmission of anxious embodiment.

Early on in my working life as a psychotherapist, I picked up the rumblings of body distress through the eating and body-image difficulties I encountered with people in the consulting room. I wrote about the ways in which, tucked into notions of thinness and fatness, were complex social and psychological ideas and feelings that were having difficulty being expressed directly. Since I wrote *Fat is a Feminist Issue* and *Hunger Strike* (1978 and 1986), the problems I sought to describe have mushroomed: eating problems and body distress now constitute an ordinary part of everyday life for many people and many families. With more and more countries entering global culture, the symbolic meanings attached to fat and thin have come to assume a shared significance for many whose recent historic concerns centred simply on getting enough food. But the 'right' food and the 'right' size now signify one's membership in modernity, while failing to get one's food and size right can signify shame, failure or a rejection of the values we are presumed to aspire to. In this context, Freud's understanding of the symbolic meanings in an individual's life has a salience, but also a limitation. The growing bodily transformations desired both individually and collectively suggest we need to marry developmental theory – how we understand the passage from infancy to adulthood – with the impact of contemporary social practices.

The last thirty years have extended our understanding of what conflicts in the mind can do to the body. They have underlined the fact that there is now a crisis about the body itself. This has made me question the whole notion of the body as something that unfolds organically according to its own genetic imprint from birth on, acted upon by the mind (and nutrition) only at key developmental stages. The body is no longer something essentially stable. New theories of psychological development are required to address the primary terrain of our human physicality and in this book I suggest ways of thinking about the body that provide, I believe, the starting points for a theory of body development just as compelling as our existing theories of the mind. When we have understood more about the psychology of our bodies – and we are learning much both from psychotherapists and body therapists and from the labs of neuro-psychoanalysts and neuro-psychologists – we will be able to propose a more fully psychosomatic theory of human development. We may also then be able to better understand the impact and the mechanisms by which the visual cortex is affected by our image-saturated culture, and how this has led to a diminution of the rich variety of human body expressions, which are disappearing rapidly. Today only a few aspirational and idealised body types which everyone feels enjoined to work towards are taking the place of differing forms of embodiment. Like the languages we are losing fortnightly,[4] we are almost doing away with body variety.

These are my clinical concerns and my theoretical propositions. At a moral level, I am pained and disquieted by the homogeneous visual culture promoted by industries that depend on the breeding of body insecurity and which then create beauty terror in so many people. Millions, literally millions, struggle on a daily basis against troubled and shaming feelings about the way their bodies appear. It is not a trivial problem just because it is a personal struggle which might be expressed as, and is sometimes mistaken for, an issue of vanity. It is far more serious than we first take it to be and it is only because it is now so ordinary to be distressed about our bodies or body parts that we dismiss the gravity of body problems, which constitute a hidden public health emergency – showing up only obliquely in the statistics on self-harm, obesity and anorexia – the most visible and obvious signs of a far wider-ranging body dis-ease.

This condition of late modernity is not inevitable. It is not the only possible outcome of a digital and hyper-saturated image culture. The very tools which have given rise to a narrowing aesthetic could be redeployed to include the wide variety of bodies people actually have. Nor is it necessarily in the long-term interests of the style industries to promote a limited aesthetic. Indeed, it may benefit these same industries to celebrate diversity and variety and to make it their ethical aim to transform the body distress so many experience today.

This book examines what is happening to bodies in our time and why. It introduces some extreme examples, while it asks the reader to review some of the very ordinary things we find ourselves doing. It presents developmental theory from the perspective of the body, showing the ways in which early family life can foster various kinds of body insecurities, creating the sense that the body we have is somehow not our true body. It discusses visual culture and the way it is affecting us and offering us a form of belonging through the personal replication of the images we see, and it looks at the way in which the visual representation of a particular kind of Westernised body is captivating young people in those countries entering modernity through globalism to take up a body that may be at odds with the body they have. The attempts by young people in Japan or Fiji, Saudi Arabia or Kenya to refashion their bodies reveal the sorrow of troubled bodies around the world. Body hatred is becoming one of the West's hidden exports.

A search for contentment focused around the body is a hallmark of our times. The varied expressions of body dissatisfaction and the search for solutions form the subject of this book. Although psychoanalysis has understood some physical symptoms as the expression of the distress of the mind, I will be arguing that physical symptoms such as eczema or adiposity are also an expression of a bodily distress in the body itself, engendered by social forces, family preoccupations and transgenerational body trauma. Why, I hope to answer, is bodily contentment so hard to find? Why are body transformations, from sex change to amputation to cosmetic surgery, if not ubiquitous, then part of public consciousness and growing in number? Why is sex a must-have, wrapped up with performance and saturated with fantasy in a way that would have Freud reeling? How might we understand the appeal of reality-TV shows which promise redemptive bodies? What is wrong with our bodies as they are and why?

By probing these questions, I hope to be able to describe and theorise the bodies of our times. Bodies, I will argue, are not in any sense matter of fact, the simple outcome of our DNA. Poised between a time when for many in the West their bodies are no longer used to produce goods and one in which replacement body parts from hair to toes and personalised medication are promised, we are trapped in confusion. What exactly *are* these bodies we are trying to live in? What kind of part of us do they constitute? How are we to relate to them? This book wants to leave the reader with an expanded understanding of our bodies, to bolster our resilience in the face of unprecedented attack and to bring sustainability to our bodies so that we can live with and from them more peaceably.

1

BODIES IN OUR TIME

Can you imagine wanting to do away with a limb because, even though you have two healthy legs, they more than annoy you – so much so that you feel misshapen or incomplete; trapped in a body that feels wrong and not how your body should be? And can you imagine living fifty years, during which time you had fathered six children, with the thought that only through a double amputation above the knees will you feel whole and complete?

Such was the dilemma of Andrew,[1] who became enamoured with the idea of becoming free of at first one leg and then the other. On finding no one to help him in his quest to rid himself of his pedal encumbrances, he turned to the internet and became part of a community of amputee wannabes.

Most people coming upon a man who wants to do away with his legs would have the immediate thought that this was disturbed and crazy. The desire feels so strange and outside of the ordinary that it is hard to set aside one's visceral response. But that is what the psychologist Dr Bert Berger succeeded in doing when Andrew consulted him in the Veterans Hospital in Milwaukee. Like any reasonable doctor, Dr Berger applied his mind to his patient's suffering. Medico-psychological ethics prevented him from offering the operation which Andrew imagined would make him feel whole. So he tried to understand the emotional state of mind that had led to this paradoxical desire.

∾

In his early writings on hysteria, Freud had proposed that strange bodily symptoms, such as a psychologically paralysed arm or the phenomenon of a patient speaking in a foreign tongue, could not only be understood but be treated. In a break with the folk-like explanations of the witches and shamans, he offered a talking cure in which, through a special kind of listening, the doctor and patient would come upon the unconscious reasons for the non-biologically based symptoms and would uncover, through talking, the dilemmas they encapsulated and the symptoms would dissolve. Freud's cases from 1895 were revolutionary and compelling. They entranced so many people to study the new science of psychoanalysis that by the time Bert Berger came to meet Andrew, psychotherapists of all persuasions had become accustomed to believing that psychological methods were the most efficacious and ethical approach to body disturbances. Were Andrew able to understand more deeply what fuelled his desires, the theory went, he would be able to avoid surgery. More specifically, if he could describe his emotional pain and the psychological picture he envisioned for himself post amputation, it might lead to a new acceptance of his body as it actually existed.

Such thinking has been sound for over a hundred years. It has helped people troubled by body disturbances to find new ways of living in and with their bodies. But tested against the desire for amputation or sex change, talking isn't always sufficient. Certainly it wasn't for Andrew. He didn't only want to talk; he wanted surgery. And he had been encouraged by reports of the work of Dr Robert Smith in Scotland, who, when faced with two similar cases, had offered amputations after concluding that this was the most humane of all possible treatments.

Even after several decades of working with people with

body difficulties, I too was intrigued by Andrew's desire for amputation. Of course it didn't just intrigue me; it also disturbed and stunned me and forced me to stretch my mind to try to imagine the circumstances that would make such desires urgent and compelling.

These days we know quite a bit about a reverse phenomenon: the physical sensations and inconveniences associated with a phantom limb – a body part that is no longer there.[2] We know of widows who, having lost their husbands, often continue to put out two coffee cups and two cereal bowls. We can understand how this occurs. Less comprehensible at first glance is the disconcerting experience of a man who endeavours to attract a waiter's attention or to answer a telephone with an arm that no longer exists. Beset by strange spectral feelings which can be both humiliating and deeply disturbing, he might fear that feeling sensations for a missing body part is a sign of madness.[3]

The widow, we can understand, is dehabituating herself, slowly unhooking herself from an identity and a long life with a husband. She doesn't always get her new reality right. Repression works to lull her into forgetfulness. The phantom limb sufferer knows that something is missing, but his body seems to act independently, as though his absent limb were still present. His mind has a kind of split: a cognitive knowledge of a physical reality and with it the continuing physical sensations of a present but absent limb. Maddening indeed, particularly before the work of Dr Vilayanur Ramachandran, sometimes nicknamed the Sherlock Holmes of phantom limbs, became widely known.

Ramachandran showed that the patients he studied were not mad at all. Their brains had made a curious adaptation to the severing: the neural pathways of the now missing arms, legs or fingers were remapped on to other areas of the body. By stimulating a specific area of the cheeks of his patients, he could duplicate the twitching, itching and cramping of absent parts and all manner of extraordinarily confusing behaviours. For marked on the facial nerves were sensors which mimicked the feelings of the previously present arm or leg.

Ramachandran's work brought relief to many. In a series of remarkable notebooks, we learn about the human body's capacities to feel what apparently is not there in more extravagant ways than we might ever imagine. For example, he describes the case of an engineer from Arkansas who, after losing his leg below the knee, felt greatly extended sensations as his orgasm swelled from his penis into the area of his phantom foot.[4]

Ramachandran's pioneering work has allowed us to see how phenomenally adaptive we are. He showed how phantom physical experiences are not imagined or mad, but have a material basis in the neuro-circuitry of the brain.[5]

Andrew's desire to rid himself of his two 'superfluous' legs poses a more mysterious problem. Ramachandran's work describes how our brains map our body schema and explains that when an area is under-stimulated following limb loss, the brain remaps the neural circuits in a way that may produce the physical sensations of the lost parts. Did Andrew's problem lie in the reverse of this phenomenon, an inability to feel his legs? Were the electrical impulses in his brain unresponsive when his legs were stimulated? No. That might have been simpler. Andrew's difficulty was that he felt his legs too amply. Amputation was his solution. But if that was the solution, where had the problem come from? How had these legs, so integral to a person's life, come to be seen as excess?

Children who feel that they are unloved can believe that

there must be something very wrong about them which makes them unacceptable. The stinging sense of being not right causes them confusion and hurt, but they do not give up the desire for love and acceptance. They despair of it, certainly. They pine for it and perhaps fear it. But their pursuit of love and acceptance will dovetail with an attempt to change themselves into someone the child himself can accept.

Neither as a child nor as an adult did Andrew feel his body was acceptable. His legs so offended him that, despite his many attempts to get help, including from Dr Berger, his capacity for self-acceptance had been too compromised. Eventually he inserted both his legs into a single support hose and then packed it with dry ice until he had cut off the circulation, so that a surgeon was forced to remove limbs which were atrophying.

We wince when we hear this. At the pain of the amputation, and at the pain of the distress which led a middle-aged man to feel that self-acceptance would elude him until his legs were severed. Such extreme behaviour seems almost unfathomable. Why and how does an able-bodied man, a man who trained in the army and thus had a rigorous physical education, reach the point where he not only wants to do away with his legs but actually does so? We also wonder how his story will turn out and if amputation will solve the problem. Will Andrew find the peace and contentment he imagined? Does life as an amputee satisfy?

We have become used to asking these sorts of questions over the last thirty years of individuals 'trapped in the wrong sex' who have begun to talk about the compelling nature of their need to change their bodies.[6] My first internship as a trainee psychotherapist was in a clinic for sentenced men considered too fragile to survive the brutality of New York

City prisons. Dressing as women and contemplating doing away with penises that felt surplus to requirements, they were judged as too challenging to the other inmates. Instead, they were put on probation and sent for therapy.

When my first patient, Michaela, wanted to turn his penis into a labia, my response, though perhaps less brutish than that of potential cellmates, was nevertheless a squeamish one. As a young feminist, bent on understanding the social and psychological processes that made us into men and women, I was both interested and uneasy. Feminism was struggling to assert that sexual biology need not define or confine us, yet I came to understand how severely Michaela felt misdefined and confined by his. He wasn't the only man. Other clinic patients, Ruby and Maria and Georgia, arrived for their appointments in clothing, shoes, handbags, jewellery and make-up that were such exaltations of femininity that I came to agree with them that the essence of who they felt themselves to be had been miscast. They were in the wrong bodies.

As my sympathy for their excruciating dilemmas grew, so my queasiness dissolved. Biology and psychology had not melded as expected. Michaela's imperative was to transform himself. He could no more live with himself with a penis than Andrew could with legs. His penis had become an impossibility, and even though neither he nor I found the words that might have helped him those thirty odd years ago, I recognised them in a 2006 interview with the actress Aleshia Brevard, who termed the male genitals she was born with 'an embarrassing often life-threatening birth defect'.

Her eloquence makes this startling statement into something so matter of fact that we are able to take note of what she says without prejudice or emotional alarm. We slow down and listen. The word 'defect' lets us imagine, along with her, 'the turmoil … the confusion with which [she] lived'[7] and which stopped her being able to find herself in a body that matched up her psychological sense of her self with her physical sense.

For Aleshia Brevard, as for Michaela, there was a tangible need to change her body. Not for her the adaptation of cross-dressers such as the Thai lady boys, the young men who masquerade as beautiful young women for the delectation of Western men whose homosexuality shames them in ways that lead them to seek out masculine bodies disguised as those of young women. Aleshia Brevard changed her sex and worked as an actor and a theatre director before becoming a writer. The correcting of a 'birth defect' was performed in the 1960s, when she was in her twenties, and it was a huge relief to her.

We find it hard to view Andrew's five decades of living with legs he'd rather live without as a similar kind of birth defect. Our imagination is too thin. Most of us dread physical impediments. We associate restricted movements, limitations on our physicality, the hunch and the hobble, with ageing, not with the promise of a new life. And yet if we think of Andrew's excess legs as psychologically akin to a transsexual's sense of being in the wrong body, we can usefully make the same kind of enquiry that we make about those who desire sex change. Where, we ask, did this desire come from? What is the family background? How did his legs assume the same kind of significance as an unwanted penis?

To get a grip on an idea that at first glance has little emotional reverberation, one can formulate a set of questions that will help us construct a picture that might illuminate the 'whys and wherefores' of Andrew's longings and actions.

Had Andrew's parents ridiculed his toddling as a child? Was he carried everywhere so that his legs represented an extra he felt he didn't need? Was he desperate to be carried but made to toddle? Did his legs represent a kind of independence he had never felt ready for? Were his parents, relatives and teachers disabled themselves? Did he feel emotionally cut off at the knees? As I wondered about all this, I tried to to put myself in his situation and scorn my own legs. I imagined myself legless. Immediately I felt awfully exposed. My sexuality felt too open to the world and my bottom too prominent. The surprise was that, at least for my momentary fantasy, neither frailty nor vulnerability was the dominant feeling. But my personal exploration could not take me very far: the situation was too foreign for me to find a resonance in myself. So I went back to questioning what it was about the totality of Andrew's body that had become an affront to him by reflecting on what was happening to bodies in 1950s America that might make amputation appear attractive.

Andrew grew up in a strained household. He describes his schoolteacher mother as harsh, his father as neglectful. A lonely unhappy child, he used to stare out of the window hoping for something to happen. Nothing much was happening in white suburban America that could capture his interest. Things were pretty much the same in one house as the next. At least it appeared that way.[8] A dreaded exception was polio: the scare of infection was rampant. Immunisation was the goal of public health. A close friend of his mother's who was kind to him limped. A child at school managed ably on crutches. A set of joyful pictures in the lush *Life* magazine – in those days an important periodical –showed children with polio playing ball. The pictures enthralled him. They provided a vibrant contrast to the bleakness of his days.

In his mind, Andrew grew a solution to his sense of being emotionally stranded: he would remake his body into one which aroused empathy – in others and in himself. He began to long for a body that exposed the wounds of feeling unlovable and unacceptable. A body that physically mirrored his emotional hurt and damage. A body that might evoke some concern. As he approached adolescence, he secretly experimented with putting one leg into the trouser leg of the other and began to use crutches in a foreshadowing of the body he would have to wait almost forty years to obtain.

Andrew's situation sets a challenge. We have learned very little if we categorise it only as an obsession, a hysterical misperception of what exists, a bizarre symptom. In so doing, we box it up, sequester our discomfort or alarm, but we haven't understood. And while we might not be able to understand immediately, if we pause and use conceptual tools as well as our discomforting feelings as a means and not as an impediment to investigation, we may be able to formulate a set of questions about bodies in our time that will have a relevance greater than Andrew's immediate dilemma.

Dr Bert Berger reports that after the amputation Andrew finally engineered, he has found a life that works for him. He has achieved a bodily contentment that previously eluded him. Perhaps it is in this sense that Dr Berger says that Andrew is not mentally disturbed, for he found in the removal of his legs a solution. It gave him a sense of having a body that was right for him. With Aleshia Brevard we get a sense that when she found a physical resolution, she experienced a quiet contentment. Having her 'birth defect' repaired early on, she has lived for many years as a woman, with the ordinary discontents that visit contemporary femininity.

Although Andrew and Aleshia felt extreme versions of body distress, they are emblematic of our focus on body ills and the way we feel we can and must work on our body as a personal project. The fact that we can transform the body makes it a site of dissatisfaction which can be overcome. The overcoming of dissatisfaction has, today, come to take centre stage. It is the focus of personal anguish, individual responsibility and political concern, especially when it comes to the body going 'fat' or being sexually active. When a British Cabinet member responsible for Children, Schools and Families erroneously compares the scourge of obesity to the danger posed by climate change without being ridiculed, we see the confusion and panic about the body today that create an ignorant and gullible stance, in this case towards the myth of obesity. Such an attitude towards the body is the stamp of our times. Our bodies are deemed out of control and must be disciplined. Eating is one manifestation, sexuality another, drinking and drugs yet others. The flip side of this attitude is that we seem to believe that almost everything about the body can be changed by the individual. Biological designation apart, pigmentation, noses, lip contours and signs of ageing are all subject to improvement. The pull to refashion comes from categorising bodies as raced – white, black, brown, Asian – and then, once raced, as classed – working-class,[9] middle-class and upper-class bodies used to look, move, dress and speak distinctively – after which each body was differentially accepted and treated depending on age, size and notions of beauty. When body or facial characteristics locate the individual in a disadvantaged group, then specific bodily characteristics engender stigma and disdain.[10] At which point an industry arises to offer the transformation of those physical markers as a way out of the designation.

Challenging discrimination and working with and on behalf of others to create social equality is a disappearing ethos. We are now exhorted to take individual responsibility for our progress and position. When this comes to the body, physical health and looking good are deemed paramount, but the individual body then becomes freighted with a weight it cannot always bear without meddling. Aided by material science, brain research, chemical potions and the fixes of the pharmacological and beauty industries, we are encouraged to see the body as a place of personal accountability and truth. How we look and the diseases we manage to avoid or contract are deemed to be our personal responsibility as well, even though most cancers, for example, are environmental. Liability for our health and beauty belongs to us. Our longings and ambitions are couched in physical terms. Bodies become our personal missions to tame, extend and perfect.

Even at the most basic level, choice is the mantra. Take reproduction. There is a recent trend among partnered heterosexual women in their mid-thirties to opt for assisted reproduction before possible fertility problems emerge. The decision to bypass sexual intercourse as a way of begetting children is argued to be sensible and effective. Simultaneously, that which used to produce children – sexuality – is visible everywhere, a commodity we are encouraged to own or produce. Devoid of moral salience, except for the obligation to always be wanting and doing it, sex becomes all things to all people. Despite the propaganda, incontinent sex is rarely conflict-free and simply pleasurable. Meanwhile acts of physical endurance, such as climbing mountains and running marathons, become morally charged and amply applauded. Their aim might be to make us feel alive. The response they draw is admiration and awe: perched on our backsides hour upon hour, many of us wonder how this physical challenge can be achieved. Of course while we are in cyber-land, we are offered unlimited scope to create fantasy bodies on screen that have almost nothing to do with our bodies as they are.

No surprise, then, that our bodies are biting back. While

we demand more rigour and have high expectations of what the fit, healthy and beautiful body can deliver for us, there is an increase in symptoms, from sexual dissatisfactions to eating problems, fear of ageing, body dysmorphia and addiction to cyber-disembodiment, which reveals how individuals struggle to make sense of the material source of their existence.

2

SHAPING THE BODY

Tony Bell wears a suit during the day but at home he cannot wait to undress and feel the air around his body. He's never been comfortable in a suit. It's too confining. Now in his sixties, Tony recalls how he spent part of his early childhood in the African veld, living among the Ndebele tribe around the area known as Matabeleland in the west of Zimbabwe, near South Africa. Until he was four years old, Tony lived an ordinary enough English middle-class family life. When his parents died during the war, he was sent to live with an aunt in what was then Rhodesia.

Tony has no memory as to how he then came to live with the nearby Ndebele tribe. Finding himself with an ill-prepared and unwelcoming relative, he either gradually spent more and more time with the tribe or ran away. For six years, until he reached the age of ten, Tony lived with the Ndebele, enjoying their way of life and their stories. To our child-centred ears, his story sounds incredible and too much like a child's fantasy of being orphaned.[1] But if we imagine a maiden aunt in a colonial outpost in the late 1940s suddenly having to raise a child without the emotional resources to do so, we can just about see how a boy who had lost his parents could be experienced as a bit of a nuisance. And then it's not such a big step to see how he might come to spend an increasing amount of time with the servants or the farm workers, so that he gradually found himself adopted into a more welcoming environment.

Tony identified with this new enlarged family, taking on the customs of his adopted tribe and learning to run fast, play in the river and listen to the storytellers. Now, fifty years on, his time with the Ndebele is blissfully idealised, in contrast to his disturbing recapture by colonial settlers. He remembers being pursued by a search party with a net, as if he were an animal, and then handed over to two comically clothed women.

We can guess how bewildering his return must have been to his maiden aunt. Washed and scrubbed down while he kicked and resisted, he was then placed indoors in a bed with white sheets that, compared to the ground he'd become used to, felt uncomfortably rough. Today, social workers and counsellors would be on hand to help Tony speak about what he had lived through and readjust to a society he had left when he was so very little. But back then, in the 1950s, he was shipped home to the UK and, in a matter-of-fact way, expected to resume life as an English boy with no guidance apart from some extra help with reading.

What I wanted to find out about from Tony was the physical footprint of his experience with the Ndebele. He joined them as a little boy in the formal English clothing of shorts, shirt, white socks and sandals and gradually switched his identification and his sense of belonging from his western parents to his clan. The period he spent with the tribe was significant. From the age of four to ten, a child is testing out his physicality on a progressively wider landscape. In the West, he'd be riding bikes, swimming, kicking footballs, playing on swings, slides and roundabouts, going camping and generally enjoying mucking about. Sartorially, post-war Britain wouldn't have offered much scope for choice and Tony would have been indistinguishable from millions of other boys of the same age dressed in the same way. But of course Tony's life had taken a bizarre turn. He was no longer an ordinary English boy. He hadn't lived in a house, bathed in running hot water, sat at a table to eat with a knife, fork, spoon and serviette. Now he had to bathe with soap, 'an offensive smell' which was alien and disorienting and distanced him from 'the smell of being'. 'Once you start using soap,' he said woefully, 'you lose your sense of smell. You can't smell what grass it is. You can't smell what time of day it is. Finally,' said Tony after a pause, 'you adapt.'[2]

But Tony Bell adapted only so far. His physicality had been formed in the context of his Ndebele companions and he had to remake it in the Midlands of the 1950s, sitting at a desk, holding a pen, playing cricket and adjusting to wearing socks and shoes and the conventional clothes of an adolescent boy. Years later, his daughter found it odd to have a father who walked around naked at home. Tony's years in Africa had formed a dissonant physical imprint for a western man. He could and did wear a suit. But to him it was only a covering and failed to provide him with a sense of belonging. Besuited, he was out of sorts. He found it difficult to sustain intimate relationships, preferring to come indoors and strip off immediately, disarming his girlfriends. Mismatched and physically uneasy, his experience reveals to us how much of what we take for granted and view as ordinary and natural about our bodies is instead evidence of the power of our specific personal environments to shape our physicality.

Reflecting on Tony's story, one thinks immediately of Victor, the 'Wild Child of Aveyron', who lived for years with animals in the woods of France, and the efforts of those who took up his cause. While some scholarship discredits the rash of unsocialised feral children being 'discovered' of late, Victor's story is not contested. In 1799, Victor was found in the countryside close to the woods of Saint-Sernin-sur-Rance and, rather like Tony Bell, was captured and brought into a household from which he twice escaped. On 8 January 1800, he emerged from the woods once again and thus began a process of his being examined, taught, quasi-socialised and exhibited – a process which was to last until the end of his life. Victor of Aveyron was of considerable interest because his appearance near Toulouse at the turn of the nineteenth century coincided with crucial Enlightenment questions about what constituted consciousness and the differences between humans and animals. These prefigured questions which have come up ever more frequently as debates about genetics and heredity, nature and nurture, have been ideologically reformulated for each subsequent generation of philosophers, policy-makers and scientists.

A young medical student, Jean Marc Gaspard Itard, tried to teach Victor the ways of the human. Victor couldn't talk. He emitted sounds. He did not stand up straight, nor could he walk. He moved in a crouched position almost on all fours, mimicking, it was presumed, the physicality of the animals among whom he had raised himself. Unlike Tony Bell, he had never learned to eat cooked food and to do so sitting at a table with plates and cutlery. His life had been in the wilds. His body temperature had adapted to cope with extremes which the socialised human animal could barely tolerate without protective clothing. Taken out into the snow naked by the eminent French naturalist Abbé Pierre Joseph Bonnaterre, Victor jumped around, appearing to greatly enjoy himself. It was not just his outward physicality that took a non-human form. Remarkably, his internal thermostat had been calibrated according to the exigencies of the outdoor life he had lived with animals. Where their animal skin and fur provided them with a built-in temperature control, his body had made an extraordinary adjustment so that it operated similarly – without the clothes we associate with mankind.

Itard, a young and dedicated doctor who had already documented the first case of Tourette's syndrome and who would go on to make his reputation in the field of hearing, spent many years trying to introduce Victor to language and speech. Thought to be about twelve when he came out of the forest, Victor was put through a rigorous education programme in an attempt to make him resemble a human being. Caught between being treated as an oddity by scientists and philosophers and as an ordinary child by Itard's housekeeper, Madame Guérin, who cared for him, Victor became the first point of reference for the next two hundred years for anyone deconstructing notions of what it means to be human.

Of course anthropologists have introduced us to the many different ways that humanity expresses itself and sociologists have alerted us to the varied lives that people growing up in the same street in Manhattan or London experience. What Victor offers us is an insight into the raw materiality of the body and the mind, and the ways in which the body is shaped by upbringing. We now know that there is a critical period for language development. If you do not learn to speak as a youngster, you may never learn to speak. The babbling-cooing between baby and mother is a proto-language developed on the way to structuring specific facial muscles: the shapes that the tongue, lips, cheek and jaw will make and the ear will process in the construction of language. The baby is repeating the sounds she or he hears. It takes a lot of practice to get your tongue, mouth, jaw and cheek muscles to coordinate and accurately reflect back what is heard.

Just try speaking a phrase from Mandarin or Xhosa. Even if these languages are in your ear, the forming of the sounds if attempted after a certain age simply doesn't work without extraordinary practice. Even diligent students will have a hard time reproducing a foreign language they have not absorbed as a child without the specific accent of their original tongue. It is easy to pick out an Israeli speaking fluent English or an Italian speaking perfect French because the maxillofacial muscles and those in the throat employed to make sounds become structured for our primary language. Yes, we can be multilingual, but unless we are introduced to several languages at an early age, the vowel sounds, the intonation and the emphases we bring to those languages will be ever so slightly off. There is a crucial difference between speaking a language and simply hearing it. The craze for language DVDs for babies to speed up their vocabulary has been shown to retard rather than advance their speaking capacities. Melodic 'conversation', in which parents act as though their baby can understand, is what fosters speech development. My own English, learned first from my American mother and my Welsh father, has the labiality of someone who has lived in both London and New York and been intimate with English and American, just as the child born of working-class parents in the late 1940s who attended a London grammar school and learned to speak like his peers adopts two speaking styles, two accents, two sets of facial gestures and mannerisms which fluctuate according to his or her audience. One physicality, one voice fits with one environment, another physicality, another voice, another intonation with a different environment. My friend has a different version. Having left South Africa at twelve, she still articulates a long 'a' sound in words, reminiscent of that country's English. She may hear the difference between her 'a' and my 'a', but she cannot easily reproduce mine. Hers is a sound print encoding her history forty years on, a marker as profound as Victor's skin temperature as he embraced the snow, the sun and the wind unprotected by clothing.

Language and skin operate in similar ways to the rest of our corporeal structuring. Let's go inside the body a little further to see how Victor, Tony Bell and all of us develop the sense of body movement. We know that it has to do with mimicry and practice and that there are idiosyncratic ways of walking that mark out an eighteen-year-old female from Bhutan[3] from a Milanese female of the same age. Globalism, as we shall see, is challenging these differences and bringing a kind of homogeneity to all matters physical, even in relatively isolated Bhutan. Nevertheless, these young women's mannerisms are still distinct and identifiable. They have apprehended that their bodies need to reflect the demeanour of their sisters, mothers and peers. So how has this happened from the inside out? How have they actually come to inhabit their specific gestures? How does watching enable one to incorporate into one's very being the physicality of one's mother, sister or friend?

Robert Sylvester, Emeritus Professor of Education at the University of Oregon, asks us to reflect on a very ordinary action between a parent and an infant. The parent sticks out her or his tongue and the baby responds with the same gesture. We might laugh seeing this and think no more about it. But 'how can an infant possibly master such a complex motor act immediately after observing it?' It's a good question. Projecting the tongue is an intricate task. While we respond delightedly to the infant's action, if we do reflect on what it takes for a baby to reciprocate our sticking-out tongue, we recognise how many processes must be occurring in the baby's mind to enable that spontaneous response. The baby has to see, then translate that seeing into an invitation to respond and then activate the muscles which control the tongue and the mouth to facilitate the tongue's extension.

If we were to look inside the brain, we would see a thin

band of cells in the motor cortex which extends from ear to ear and is activated when movement occurs. In front of the motor cortex, closer to our forehead, we'd see action in the pre-motor cortex, the area that prepares for the movement. A chance observation by Giacomo Rizzolatti and Vittorio Gallese in a laboratory in Parma, where they were studying monkeys just over a decade ago, led to the naming of a new class of neurons which are involved in this dual phenomenon of seeing and doing. Rizzolatti and Gallese were tracking the firing of brain cells as monkeys stretched their arms out to reach for peanuts. They were interested in what happened in the monkeys' brains when this movement was made. They observed that every time the monkeys reached for a peanut, a specific group of cells in the frontal lobes fired. One day, a scientist from another lab came in to see Rizzolatti and Gallese and casually picked up one of the peanuts. Rizzolatti and Gallese were astonished to see that the same cells that were fired when the monkeys picked up a peanut fired when the monkeys saw the man picking one up.[4] The act of seeing the scientist pick up a peanut induced the same neural behaviour in the monkeys, as if they were performing the same action themselves. This extraordinary and unexpected result implied their brains mirrored the movements the monkeys saw whether or not they were making the movement themselves.

Many experiments on – including some involving humans observing other humans in action[5] – this group of cells was named and designated as the mirror neuron system. When we watch another human being making a movement, whether it is sticking out a tongue, carrying packages, swerving, dancing, eating or clapping their hands, our neurons fire in the same way, as if we ourselves were making the movement. From the brain's perspective, Rizzolatti and Gallese found, watching is pretty similar to doing. The brain has a built-in empathic and mimicking capacity. It translates what is seen through the eyes into the equivalent of doing and is structured to absorb and prepare itself for what we may not yet have mastered.

This discovery tells us that the brain of the observing infant is structuring the sense of movement before she or he has the capability to move. Although the mirror neuron cell has not yet been found in humans, there is a mirror system in which the ensemble of millions of cells at a time is implicated in the capacity to learn how to move by observation before one has made the movement. The mirror system operates in all spheres, whether we are watching sport, being a back-seat driver or feeling the emotions an actor portrays on stage or screen. Victor's gait was literally copied as well as neurally encoded in the mirror neurons. We can speculate that Andrew's recasting of a legless body as right for him involved some mirror neuron activity as he watched the family friend and the boy in school hobble about. He was captivated by their movements and we can imagine that he 'applied' their bodies to his body and experienced a forty-year-long desire which may have become expressed neurally as much as psychologically. And so it is for all of us. The particular gestures and movements of a parent or a sibling form a visual/neural template. This explains why children's mannerisms so often reflect those of parents. It is not so much genes that are at play as visual exposure. We can see this vividly in young people who seem effortlessly to flick their hair like Rachel in *Friends* or imitate the poses of models or African-American rappers. They don't have to practise mimicry for hours. By watching, they have already absorbed the feel of the movement, the idea of the look they should be achieving, without necessarily knowing it. Consider, too, the young woman who wears the hijab at home but takes it off as she joins her non-Muslim friends. She has two body stances that she has incorporated which express the different cultural sub-groups within which she lives. We see this flexibility most magnificently in actors who provide an emotional-physical representation of their character.[6] Actors are able to feel themselves into someone else's skin and convey this embodiment to us. It is how they make us believe in the character they are playing. As they do it, they are activating neural structures which have already coded these actions inside them. The mirror neuron system, then, enables us to relate at a deep level to one another. It allows us to see in the face of another what she or he is experiencing and then to have a corresponding feeling ourselves.[7]

Mirror neurons, occurring at a micro level, are thus part of the story of how we come to have a body sense. Psychoanalytic researchers such as Beatrice Beebe and Miriam and Howard Steele have shown how we learn about who we are in a mental and physical sense through having our own bodies and minds reflected back to us. They have unpicked what occurs frame by frame between a mother and her infant to show us what a very delicate and at the same time a very ordinary process this is. Parents and carers respond to their babies and reflect back to their babies what they see in her or him. But what do they see in their babies? And what did I see in my babies, and in those of my dear friends, which may or may not have been there?

The baby reaches out to captivate us.[8] The baby looks at us and we look at the baby. The face-to-face contact between a parent and a baby is arresting. Each is absorbing the other. The parent becomes the baby's world and the baby becomes the parent's world. The mutual gaze does not look dissimilar to that of couples falling in love. Their eyes are fixed upon each other, and just as the courting couple are profoundly reorienting their individual worlds to accommodate one another, to take in the adoration reflected in their loved one's eyes and to give that adoration in return, so with the baby, we melt and expand ourselves to find a place for the new arrival in our inner familial world. We insert our family links into what has now become the centre of our lives: the baby. We then ascribe to our babies, attributes of other family members – Grandpa's eyebrow or Mum's fingers – and in this way we personalise and animate the baby for ourselves. We convey this sense of their welcome and their fitting into the family in such a way that the baby is now experienced as a living body and mind.

What exactly does this mean and how is it achieved? This ordinary and, as I said, delicate activity is conveyed to a baby who is not yet formed and who is being formed in the process of being related to. The baby's personality and physicality are potentials. How we engage with them, and the parts of ourselves which we offer up, create the physical and mental ambience through which the baby develops.

Parents do many things when they are relating with an infant: they respond to how the baby is, they initiate contact, play and care that are appropriate to the baby and, importantly, they bring an imaginative sense of who the baby can be to their relationship. The baby is both a real baby and a baby that lives in the imaginations, hopes and of course fears of her or his parents and those she or he grows up with. For a baby to thrive she or he has to be more than fed and kept clean. She or he needs to be held and to be engaged with as a living baby. This last thought might sound a bit mad. Of course a baby is alive. But if a baby receives only perfunctory care, if her or his needs for food and water and changing are met in a production-line manner, as happened for the many abandoned babies in the Romanian orphanages after Ceaușescu was toppled, she or he may not thrive; she may die.

In the 1940s René Spitz, the Hungarian-born psychiatrist and psychoanalyst, spent time at a hospital caring for wartime orphan babies. He reported that those babies in the hospital ward who received the same feeding and changing but were closest to the nurses' station and received a few more touches from the passing nurses survived more frequently than those furthest away, who failed to thrive. The babies who received a modicum of personal contact – who were noticed and related to by the nursing staff – survived physically and psychically. They absorbed the will to live. Those without this contact did not.

Spitz went on to compare babies raised by mothers in a penal institution who had their mothers' attention during the first year of life with babies who were raised in a foundling hospital and had less than an eighth of an individual nurse's attention. He discovered that the babies in the penal institutions fared better. The foundling babies, missing physical and emotional bonding, became easily ill or had skin diseases such as eczema and showed key development lags in their capacity to move and to speak. Although they were kept physically clean and warm and were fed nutritious food, once the months of breastfeeding (provided often by wet nurses) had ceased, their physical and mental aliveness took a downturn, with appalling consequences for their development.

A decade later, Harry Harlow, an American psychologist trained at Stanford University, became fascinated by social development. Working with monkeys, he demonstrated that both a sense of touch and warmth were crucial for bonding. Baby rhesus monkeys separated from their mothers and fed on tiny bottles became attached to the soft gauze pads that covered the floors of their cages. They 'clung to these pads', engaging in 'violent temper tantrums' when the gauze pads were removed and replaced, not unlike human infants who can also display terrible upset if their treasured bit of material or animal is dropped. The monkeys whose cages had wire floors and no gauze pads had considerable difficulty surviving during the first five days. So Harlow made a terry cloth mother monkey warmed by a light bulb which radiated heat and found that the baby monkeys could cling to it and were calm and warm.[9] Although today we might find his work ethically controversial because he removed the baby monkeys from their mothers at birth, his discovery of the significance of warmth and the capacity to touch and cling is important. It links in with the work of Rizzolatti and Gallese and Spitz, who in their very different ways illuminate how central a palpable physical relationship is in the making of the body. In their research projects they demonstrate the ways in which our bodies are shaped and structured according to the treatment we receive and what we observe. Harlow and Spitz were specifically interested in the emotional and mental development of their subjects, but thinking of their research from a body perspective I believe it tells us much about the fundamental need for physical contact and for proximity.

In the last twenty years or so, the significance of human touch, which their research hints at in different ways, has come to the fore as being crucial to psychological well-being.[10] Touch is the most basic and fundamental of human experiences. Before we can suckle, before we can even see, we are enveloped by the welcoming arms of our mother. As we nestle into her body, feel the steadiness of her heartbeat, breathe her smell, we embed ourselves with her as our beacon. Her body, her voice, her skin, her touch become the way we orient ourselves as we make our personal journey through infancy, childhood and beyond. And touch is among the most crucial of these elements, not only providing us, in the case of loving touch, with a sense of security and ease in our bodies, but shaping our biology and our neurocircuitry in ways that will affect our tempers and our personalities throughout our lives.

One of the serendipitous discoveries of the late 1980s, made in the low-tech environment of Bogotá, Colombia, where financial constraints meant a shortage of incubators for premature babies, was that the placing of the baby high on a parent's tummy with her or his ear near to the parent's heart for several hours a day, reduced the mortality rate from 70 to 30 per cent. Kangarooing, as this practice has come to be known since neonatalogists Edgar Rey and Hector Martinez described it, has been taken up widely, and skin-to-skin holding between mothers and fathers and premmies is now commonplace in neonatal environments. Apart from providing the expected bonding between the parents and the baby, this bodily contact aids subsequent breastfeeding, reduces respiratory distress and, interestingly, provides evidence of the relational potential of regulating the premature baby's temperature system. Mothers show thermal synchrony with their babies. Measuring the body temperature of mothers and babies in kangarooing mothers revealed that, when a baby became cold, the mother's body temperature would almost instantly warm up to provide greater warmth for the baby.[11] Similarly a kangarooing mother whose baby was hot could lower her own chest temperature quickly to cool the baby down. The thermal regulation the baby acquires by full term could be aided in the premature baby through this specific kind of skin-to-skin holding.

We are accustomed to thinking of our bodies as just existing, propelled to grow by reasonable nutrition and our genetic inheritance. But my experience as a psychotherapist working with people with troubled bodies shows that the kind of touch we receive when we are little and the impact of a mother's (or carer's) physical sense of herself are crucial to the development of our own body sense. Our bodies are a lot more than an executed blueprint given by our DNA.

Every gesture we make, the very way we move, our grace or lack of it, our physical confidence or unease, reflect both the country and local culture we have grown up in and the particular interpretation of our gestures that our mothers and those close to us have passed on. They do this by giving us our specific bodily gestures and guides to movement every bit as much as they give us the specific words and language with which to communicate. Every aspect of our body sense embodies something about our mother's own physicality. If she is awkward and physically reticent, we pick that up. If she is bold or intrusive, our personal body sense will accommodate that in some form. If she fails to touch us in a firm yet gentle manner, we may become confused or fearful about our bodily sensations. We might not know where our body begins and where it ends. We have all had the experience of another butting up too close and an ensuing wish to then take a step back. It is not going too far to suggest that such individuals lack a firm sense of where their body stops and so any other body in the vicinity can be pulled in to provide a proxy body boundary.[12] In the worst of cases, we may not feel that our bodies really belong to us – we will look at them as though from the outside, as a project we have to work on.

A psychologist colleague adopted ten-year-old Gina, who had been in a depressive and difficult family until she was three before being fostered unsuccessfully several times. She was causing concern for social services until she came to live with Wendy, who was by that time fifty and had never had a baby.

Gina was a prickly little thing. Punchy and cheeky, she dressed in the manner of an angry and precocious adolescent: she had deliberate ladders in her tights, spiky gelled hair and clothes that clashed. She was easy to love but she was explosive. The mixture riled Wendy and sent her back to her textbooks to see how to calm both their nerves. Gina had been hit constantly as a little girl and had found herself in fights at kindergarten and school. When she came to Wendy, she dressed as a toughie and flung herself about whenever she became frustrated. She was more than a handful.

In a study of mothers suffering from postnatal depression, Professor Vivette Glover from Imperial College School of Medicine discovered that offering baby-massage classes to depressed mothers benefits both mothers and their infants. By learning how to give loving touch they become responsive to their babies' cues, develop confidence in handling their babies and feel better themselves. While it is reasonably obvious that a friendly, caring environment with a warm teacher guiding new mums would produce a positive-feedback loop between mothers and babies, what is surprising is the finding that it is the actual *physical* process of touching which raises the level of an important bonding hormone, oxytocin, thereby laying down neural responses that will enable babies who might otherwise have been at risk, to be receptive to easy soothing, calming and closeness.

By contrast, those babies exposed to excess or unrelieved stress, intermittent physical relating or touch of a more brutal kind have lower levels of the hormone oxytocin. In place of the bonding hormone, they have raised levels of the stress-related hormone called cortisol. Primed with cortisol on a regular basis, a person is biologically and psychologically readied to seek out stress. The effects can be permanent. Ironically, the way that stress is relieved in someone with high cortisol levels is by increased stress rather than less. With heightened stress, the body's own soothing opiates kick in. Cruelly, tightly coiled individuals can't get relief until they become really uptight. They seem driven to seek ever more tension (sometimes self-generated) to overcome their normal stress threshold. Only then is there relief, generated by the body's natural narcotising system.

And so it was with Gina. She'd been pulled about and kicked as a little one and at the end of a long fighting sequence she would eventually find relief. She took this neural behavioural imprint with her as she developed, almost provoking those around her to restrain her, which only caused her to experience more aggro and to want rough physical engagement. Wendy, her new mother, was a pacifist. She believed in a benign model of child-rearing. Skilled in helping others deal with disruptive children, she was disappointed that she couldn't quite seem to make contact with Gina unless they played at boxing or, if Gina got herself into severe enough scrapes, Wendy was called into her school to take her home. Disciplining her new daughter seemed to make matters worse. If she gave her time-out in her bedroom, Wendy would return to find Gina's clothes thrown across the room and her new and favoured toys broken. Gina's body seemed to crave tension and calming hot chocolate drinks or promises of a new bike failed to interest her.

The two of them couldn't find a rhythm. They were both in despair. More than once, Wendy thought she must have made a mistake in taking on such a challenge. She longed for a little girl who she could caress and cuddle and sing to sweetly. She felt resentful and guilty. She knew raising a girl with Gina's background would be hard, but she had got on so well with her students and her own clients and in helping other mothers that she was unprepared for such frustration with Gina. It undermined her.

A year into their time together Gina entered puberty. Wendy thought matters couldn't get worse and she wondered how wise the adoption workers had been to place Gina with her. Gina was too damaged and hurt, too disappointed with adjusting to this carer and that carer who in the end would abandon her – or so it seemed to Gina – and no amount of talking helped Wendy to reach her and offer any solace or security.

Wendy explained about periods, which Gina professed to know all about, but the wry humour Wendy brought to a discussion of the various sanitary devices on offer made Gina laugh. Wendy was menopausal and the two of them found the beginnings of a more intimate physical and emotional relationship around their discussion of the vagaries of the female cycle and its allied hygiene practices.

One school morning when she was twelve, Gina, who now had long brown hair, brought a hairbrush to her mother and asked her to comb her hair and to make it into a French plait. This radical request from a rather rough and tumble girl delighted Wendy, who started to brush Gina's hair tenderly, leaving the more intricate task of a French plait for the evening after she had consulted a hairdressing manual to work out how to do it.

Thus began a new phase in their relationship in which every morning Gina and Wendy would spend almost an hour – they got up extra early to do so – preparing Gina's hair in a style that she wanted. Kirby grips sticking out of her mouth, Wendy sat on a high stool in front of a full-length mirror, while Gina sat on a short one in front of her and leaned back into her knees. They had found an intimate physical activity which satisfied them both. They talked a little as Wendy brushed Gina's hair gently and began to massage her shoulders. Gina softened and Wendy finally had the physical emotional experience of mothering her girl. The love (and, by implication, the oxytocin) began to flow between the two of them, and although Wendy wasn't about to interrupt their time together to take a reading of Gina's hormone levels, it was clear that these daily sessions were instituting a psycho-chemical change in Gina, and doubtless in Wendy too, as they found a way to interweave bodily and develop a relationship of physical and emotional trust.

Gina's ingenious initiative instigated a process by which touch, first at one remove and then more intimately, created a rich physical relationship between daughter and mother. Wendy got what few mothers of adolescents can hope for, the chance to be physically close and tender, while Gina received, perhaps for the first time, consistent and reliable safe touch which put in place for her a new template for closeness and soothing.

It is nearly always the case that, if we can notice them, the hints that patients bring are prompts towards our being able to help them heal. It is easier in a consulting room, where the task is to repair what has gone wrong and where the therapist has mechanisms and techniques for dealing with what has gone awry. In the context of a home which may evoke feelings from earlier and unhappier homes, it isn't easy to trust. Part of what adopted or fostered children automatically do (perhaps in part to familiarise themselves with their new surroundings, but mainly because that is what human beings do as we transfer understandings and feelings from one set of circumstances to another) is to inscribe on a current situation what they have learned from an earlier family setting. If their first family or families were difficult, that is what will be remembered, expected and projected on to the situation even if it isn't now the case. Gina's daring to bring Wendy a hairbrush and trust that something good could happen was received by Wendy with just the right amount of tenderness and seriousness. She took it as her opening, even though by then she too was thinking: if only I could give up!

As adults, we can know from experience how important touch feels – and not just sexually. Holding, stroking, caressing are as good to give as to receive. But we've become rather confused of late. The British are conventionally regarded as physically and emotionally buttoned up, and the horrors of paedophilia and inappropriate sexual touch between adults and children have added to our wariness about whether touching is all right or not. But even outside Britain, in the United States, teachers pick up injunctions against touching lest it be misunderstood and some dads are worrying about spontaneous physical touch with their daughters. Meanwhile at the end of a dinner party we don't know whether we are supposed to be kissing those we've just met goodbye. And if so, is it once, or twice, or do we do it three times like the Dutch?

In my consulting room a middle-aged woman described visiting her eighty-seven-year-old mother in hospital: 'She was so vulnerable. I wanted to hug her and I just couldn't. I just couldn't.' Her mother's emotional frailty made her want to touch her but she felt a coldness in her bones. Her own lack of having been held when she was a child kept her frozen.

In the bleak days of their first year together, when Wendy would imagine Gina as a teenager, she saw a tough urban child marking her identity with extreme body piercing, extensive tattoos and aggressive clothing. She wondered how she would

manage to accept such an external manifestation of tough-
ness in a daughter of hers who was clearly so very vulnerable.
How would she find a way to accept her style and give her a
sense of being appreciated? She feared she'd be walking around
with a girl who proclaimed her dissatisfactions and that Gina's
appearance would invite hostility in return. Yes, she felt over-
protective, and with good reason. She knew that a multiply
fostered girl could be drawn to other troubled youngsters and
live on the edge. She worried that she would not be able to
provide enough of a counterbalance to the dangers that would
attract Gina. So it was a delightful and reassuring surprise
when the fourteen-year-old Gina softened further and began
to dress in the same kinds of clothes as the rest of her class-
mates. She experimented with looking tough, but that was
only one kind of outfit; more and more she gravitated towards
a look that said she fitted in and was no longer an outcast.
As her inside physicality was becalmed, so her body relaxed
and, feeling safer within it, she could give clothing and pos-
tural messages of ease and developing confidence. The way she
was in her body and her clothing solicited pleasure in others.
She received back a respect which further enhanced her. From
outside to inside and inside to outside, Gina was physically
and psychologically remaking herself through her relationship with Wendy. She was growing a new internal body.

3

SPEAKING BODIES

Sam was six when he came to live in his foster family. A scrawny pale-faced nervous little boy, he was thrown into a hurly-burly family with a loving new mum and dad and two older teenage children starting their journey into adulthood. Mum couldn't have been kinder. She'd opened her modest house to scores of children through the years. Some had stayed just a few days or months, some a couple of years. Sam was nearly thirteen when I met him, although he only looked about nine. Mum was who you'd really want to be adopted by if you had come from hell: a big comfy woman in her forties with a generous lap and heart. She was intelligent and thoughtful, someone whose confidence made it seem that life might just be possible, however hopeless it felt at the moment.

Anne was the ablest foster mother Kent County Council had on their books and over the past twenty years they'd sent her 130 children from the most anguished of circumstances. She always came through for the children, even if she suffered heartbreak herself when it was time for them to leave her. This was especially the case for a little baby, Ethan, who'd been severely mistreated for the first six weeks of his life and who came to her with two fractured legs which his birth mother had twisted and broken. Once out of plaster, baby Ethan was rigid and brittle. He couldn't bear to be held or touched. The whole family sang him soothing lullabies. Anne began to stroke his baby legs softly with a furry bunny rabbit. Slowly, slowly, he unfurled and, like Gina, who allowed her hair to be brushed, this baby found an object, not part of Anne and not part of himself, which became the conduit for some loving physical attention. Soon he was able to be stroked by Anne's hands and then cuddled. By the time he was some five months into the placement he started to smile.

But unlike Ethan, Sam's 'recovery' from his tormented background proved long and difficult. He had come to her at a later stage of development and Anne and social services were concerned about his lack of physical growth. For several years he was put under the care of a paediatrician who prescribed growth hormones. They didn't produce the expected result. It was as though Sam's body was determined not to grow. With skilled therapeutic help, Anne tried to find words to speak to him of what she had heard about the sexual violation he had experienced from his birth mother's boyfriend. He recoiled from hearing about it and he certainly didn't know how to talk about it himself. Trapped in a closed-down state in which he seemed to be blocking out what had happened to him, his physical processes almost imploded in stasis. Anne wondered what could bring him out of it. She felt that if she could keep open the possibility of talking to him about what had happened and explain to him that the abuse hadn't been his doing, he might unfreeze.

Listening to Anne and meeting Sam, I tried to make sense of what could be going on inside Sam's unconscious mind that could so fundamentally thwart his growth. Imagining him as a confused and violated six-year-old removed from his mother, who, despite her failure to protect him, was his security, it made sense that he would be terrified. Not having words for what had happened and was happening could make anyone close down. But what could explain his stunting? How could we understand that?

As Sam wasn't my case, I did not have access to the tools

available to me when working with a patient. I know people often think that psychoanalysts are analysing them in social situations but that is not the case. Psychoanalytic understanding comes from the special conditions of the consulting room and the analytic relationship. That is when it is at its strongest and most convincing. Nevertheless, when I met Sam and Anne in the course of my research I couldn't but help speculate and conjecture. Had Sam's development been irrevocably eroded by his early treatment? Was it possible that if Sam lived long enough in a secure and protected environment he would feel safe enough to grow again? Did he have some notion that his growing had caused the problems in the first place? Did he worry that if he grew he too would turn into a man who hurt children? Did he hope that if he didn't grow he could go back to his birth mother as the little boy she had lost? These kinds of questions and their possible answers were not addressed but they would certainly have been in the minds of those helping Anne to enable Sam to grow and would have formed part of a conversation with him when he might be more able to consider his body's fierce mutiny. For now, though, his foster mother accepted Sam's lack of physical progress as an enigma and a sorrow and loved him for the little boy he continued to need to be.

In my own practice, I am quite accustomed to experiencing what I can only describe as wildcat sensations in my own body. When that occurs, I know that there is a fair chance that I am receiving an unconscious transmission of some physical state that cannot easily be felt by the person I am working with. I am not alone in this. Psychotherapists rely on being able to pick up feelings from their patients. It is a guide to aspects of their patients' experience which need to be addressed and so they get presented in ways that, to a non-therapeutically oriented ear, seem most odd. Perhaps you know what I mean: you are with someone who seems quite interesting but you feel unexpectedly sleepy. Or perhaps you are talking in an animated way but suddenly you find yourself feeling stupid. There is nothing overt, nothing to pinpoint in the conversation, but subtle feelings cross the ether and your enthusiasms melt away, leaving you enervated.[1]

In therapy, these kinds of changes in mood and feelings are used by the psychoanalyst as clues. A mutual mood is not a cause for interrogation.[2] It is expected. When, however, the therapist registers an unexpected shift of mood in herself when she is with a patient, she begins a private inner dialogue with herself as to what it might mean. First she checks herself out, as though she is an object of study. What does the patient evoke in her? Why did she feel uptight just then? Why did she feel sad when the patient was making a light remark? Did the patient hit a particularly personal nerve? Such emotional states, which the therapist notices in herself, are called the countertransference. As she cordons off the feelings and reflects on them, their dissonance alerts her: something difficult needs understanding. Her body, her emotional state, become a stethoscope-like instrument for hearing what might be askew.

The first time I experienced such a wildcat countertransference in my own body, I was working with Herta, a forty-year-old violinist from Limburg. Herta's neat and calm bearing gave no hint of her extremely troubled body. But it had always been so. It was forever ill. It hurt. It ulcerated.

Herta had grown up in post-war Germany, with the pall of poverty saturating her parents' experience. They had lived through two world wars. Her story is a vivid example of how parental discomfort is absorbed and fashioned by the child. As a baby she had sicked up some of her feed. This behaviour alarmed her mother, who wanted to make absolutely sure her daughter got enough milk at each feed and who did not know that 'positing' is a perfectly ordinary thing for a baby to do. Mother felt rejected and worried and transmitted something of her dismay to Herta, who was simply dribbling back the little excess milk she did not need.

In time, the emotional inflection of the slight overfeeding and her mother's anxiety that Herta might be hungry and that she was an inadequate mother combined with Herta's attempt to regulate the amount she could ingest and a habit of involuntary vomiting developed. It was frequent enough that when Herta was five her mother took her to Frankfurt to see a psychologist who was practising the new behavioural therapy. In the empty dining room at the clinic, the psychologist fed Herta. When she threw up, he caught her vomit in a basin and made her eat it. This cruel treatment stopped her vomiting. Shortly after, however, she found another body-based symptom to express her bodily distress. She became a bed-wetter and by the time I met her she had been suffering with ulcerated colitis since her twenties.[3]

Sitting with Herta in a session about two years into her therapy, I was drawn to an unfamiliar body experience of my own. I felt suffused with a deep physical pleasure, as though I were a purring pussycat. Every part of me felt alive and contented in a way I had never been aware of before. Perhaps this is what the Buddhists call Nirvana. I am not sure. I wasn't conscious of having been dissatisfied before that moment; indeed I wasn't especially aware of my body at all. My attention had been on Herta and the hurt her body was to her.

Reflecting on this blissful purring state, I began to ask myself what was going on. What was Herta communicating to me? What was she creating in me? What was she wanting from my body? What did I want for her? Herta already had a quasi-external body, her violin, on which, with her bow, she could create the most soulful and exquisite sounds. Her perfection of that little wooden instrument, whose sensuous contours resemble the curves of a woman, could be seen to symbolise the loving parts of her mother's attention, the part of Herta that was alive and that refused the legacy of body distress. I parked my purring feeling as I thought some more about Herta's body and her symptoms.

Herta's relationship to her own body was twofold. It was an object to her and it was a trouble to her. She had no experience of just living in it. She knew her body – which was an 'it' to her – by its burdensome nature. She continually had to attend to it, whether dealing with the ungracious symptoms of loose, sometimes bloody and urgent bowel movements or the severe abdominal cramping that characterises colitis. By focusing temporarily on my contented purring body, I was able to address the 'it', the body as a body. What can I mean? The body as a body?

For a century of psychoanalysis, the axiom has been that the mind influences the body and that by excavating the conflicted thoughts associated with a symptom, the symptom would dissolve. Freud and Breuer had written about their casework with hysterical patients. They had developed the talking cure as a treatment to realise and release the unconscious ideas that had become transferred on to an hysterical symptom. In Sam's not growing, we can see if not the particulars then the outlines of this understanding of the emotional reasons for his body's shutdown. But Herta's case and, more especially, my purring response to her made me want to focus on what her body was needing in its own right. The troubled physicality induced in Herta by her mother's alarm at her early feeding response had developed into a body ill.

Herta suffered from a particularly acute body hatred. This was no ordinary body hatred of the kind we see today among so many women, young and old. Structured into the most basic aspects of her physicality was a sense of her body not being all right. In this, she was like Andrew, the man who had been desperate to rid himself of his legs. Both rejected their actual physicality, Herta through the protest that was her vomit and Andrew through seeking to remake his body without legs. Clinically, I believed I needed to be able to enter directly into the hatred Herta had of her body. Forced to swallow her protest, she came to distrust and hate what emanated from her body. And it was my belief that unless we could face the fact that her body existed for her only as hated and help her be inside the depth of that feeling, she would not be able to relinquish or transform this sense of it. Her dilemma was that in acknowledging how hate permeated her body sense, she would be stranded inside extreme distress. She would have no exit point; nor would she have a way of caring for her body.

Herta's colitis was unstable. It would come and it would almost go. Suffering from colitis meant that she could never be far away from paying heed to her body's demands. To still it, she would try various food regimens thought to be helpful. She would take care on tour that she had her medicines. She always knew where the toilets were and tended to herself as though the colitis was an object that needed looking after. She was continuously on alert. Paradoxically, the nuisance and burden of her colitis functioned as a means to self-care. This trouble-some symptom both allowed and forced her to pay attention to herself. In a roundabout way, a symptom is a mechanism (what analysts call a compromise formation) by which that which one wishes to disregard forces itself into awareness by demanding attention.

So to the purring sensation, something I was to experience, intermittently, for many months during Herta's sessions. I came to see this countertransference feeling as Herta cueing me into what she needed. In order to give up her sense of living in a hated body, Herta had created for the two of us in the room a body which felt amply comfortable and alive. It was as though she were starting all over again, only this time with a maternal analyst figure not plagued by memories of poverty and war and anxiety about feeding, but a maternal substitute who sat contentedly and calmly. Her ingenuity had conjured up what she needed. She couldn't give herself a neutral body, let alone a wondrously happy one, but she could evoke one in me, in the hope that I could then bestow it on her.

It sounds quite bizarre that Herta was able to create in me the sense of purring bodily contentment. However, psychotherapists are very used to feeling a particular kind of 'emotional health' during sessions. Therapy works, in part, because a therapist's emotional presence becomes a kind of auxiliary psyche which is used by the patient in the process of deconstructing and reconstructing their own disturbing mental state. You could think of what occurs as crudely akin to being a kind of good parental stand-in, a supportive self that – held by the therapeutic relationship – provides emotional security. With Herta it was my body's turn to become an auxiliary. And in the therapeutic space, I found that she had invoked in me this purring, reliable and solid body in her quest to find a new, more trustworthy body for herself, which she did in time develop.

Many will wonder why therapy can take so long. Why can't pain, once understood and engaged with, allow for a speedy rewrite of a physical or mental template and thus bring quick relief? It is frustrating. Our brains seem to work so fast to grasp things and yet so slowly to change. A way to think about this is to remind ourselves that the human animal has a long gestation period outside the womb, during which the baby absorbs and personalises that which will make it human. If we use language as a model and recognise that it takes a good two to four years for language to become personal and a part of oneself, then the idea that therapy is akin to absorbing a new language, only more so, begins to make sense. In therapy the patient has to unlearn one way of being and develop another, more sustainable one. This process can easily double the time it takes to acquire a new language and its idiomatic ways, making a long period of therapy essential in enabling Herta, for example, to confront her damaged and hated body and to begin to find her way to a new, more satisfying or at least medically and emotionally neutral embodiment.

Herta's struggle alerted me to the significance of early experience in the making of a body sense. Like my fellow psychotherapists, I had always taken the research literature by René Spitz, or the many studies which showed differential physical treatment of baby girls and baby boys, as evidence for the emotional structuring of girls and boys from infancy on; not, as Freud had suggested, at four, when Oedipal issues emerge. Studies showed that boys were breastfed for longer, that each feeding period was lengthier, that they were weaned later, potty-trained later and even held more than girls; and this confirmed the emotional experience of the feminine psychology. It made sense. If, because of gender inequality, girls received less nurture from infancy onwards, their feelings of entitlement would be more limited and circumscribed. From a more physical perspective, it is clear that the historical training of girls to be demure and boys to be adventurous affected their bodies' structures. It is not just biology but physical handling, physical expectation and the physical relationship between parent and child that shape girls' and boys' experience of their bodies.

In the first days of life, the patterns of sleep and feeding are regulated by that of our care-giver. Nannies, maternity night nurses, grandmas and health visitors all offer advice on how to establish a rhythm of sleeping and eating to settle the baby. This is a bio-physical emotional structuring of the baby which we tend to think unfolds naturally. But if we look from the perspective of how bodies are made, we can see that during the very early life of a baby, his or her physicality is being shaped and coaxed in ways which will create his or her actual physicality and inner sense of his or her own body.

Our bodies are made both in a literal physical sense and in a feeling sense. What we eat, how we eat, whether the food is mashed up, presented to us as exciting or fed to us by a distracted or anxious carer, whether we are held warmly or gruffly or not much held, whether we are tickled or caressed, changed frequently or not often enough: the many variants in the ways we are related to form the physical ambience of our upbringing and shape the bodies we are. There is no already pre-given body – that is too simplistic. Every body is made with the intimate imprint of the familial body story. A mother who wants her daughter to feel confident aims to convey that in her treatment of her daughter's body, but of course if she herself is physically reticent some trace of that will come through despite her efforts. The many-layered desires and actuality of the mother's own body experience are brought to her daughter as she consciously tries to shape her daughter's body in ways that are different from her own. Inside her growing daughter's body sense will reside imprints of her mother's feelings about her own body as well as her experience of how her mother felt and handled her developing body. The situation gets more complex when the daughter comes to mother her own daughter, for she will discover that she has inside her the gestures of her own mothering, which will incline her to move and act in specific ways, some of which she will be aware of and some of which are quite outside her consciousness. This complex intertwined cocktail of physical engagement is what creates our personal idiosyncratic and unique body. And shot through the individual familial body story of how we have been physically treated and treat our children is the cultural body story which both parents and children live through. Everything in our early experience shapes our bodies. Every culture marks the bodies of its people in specific ways and we see the various external markers, from the rings which extend the necks of Burmese women to the hand gestures of the Italian speaker to the way we wear our clothes, are sequestered during menstruation, or do our ablutions. We cannot see inside one another's bodies, but from the outside we can see some of the signs of how the individual's body is structured. There is also what we can measure. Public health and epidemiology have given us the tools to understand how nutritional patterns structure physical possibilities, from height to diabetes. From the outside, we can and do read people's bodies. Bodies communicate. Often, though, what we read from the body we translate into the terms of the mind.

It couldn't be otherwise, for we don't have the conceptual or linguistic vocabulary to discuss or conceive of ourselves as psychosomatic beings. The legacy of the Cartesian duality makes it hard to get our minds around the idea that our bodies are made. We wonder what that can mean. We can accept that our minds are the outcome of a variety of influences, including the familial, the peer group and the culture we grow up in.

Consider, for instance, the recent research demonstrating that immunity to childhood leukaemia is increased by babies going to day care or being in social groups.[4] This is significant because it shows how our personal physical immunity is influenced by the way we are brought up. When we discuss our upbringing or how we are raising our own children with others, we notice subtle differences in physical regimes and practices: some of us will expose our children to dirt, other people will not, some to German measles and so on. Many of these choices will structure our children's physicality, having either an immediate or a long-term effect. But when it comes to conceptualising our bodies in this way, we falter intellectually. Even in a research group such as the Body Attachment Group,[5] which explores the ways in which a body sense and the specific kinds of body awareness are conveyed to the baby in the mother–daughter relationship, we have to work hard to describe what transpires between mothers and daughters that can be seen from DVD images. We stumble to describe what we see because we are unaccustomed to this kind of focus on the body. We know it exists. We observe it, and results from other scientific fields bear out the significance of a mother's physicality on that of her child. It is striking that while almost everything we see on the DVDs can be described as being about physical exchange, we in the Body Attachment Group make an automatic translation to the psychological. We have to pull ourselves back in order to describe the physical interchange in its own terms. We look at a sequence in which the mother smiles, the baby smiles back, the mother snuggles her and the baby gets excited and flaps her arms. Mum smiles again and a circle of positive engagement occurs which we term 'attunement' – being on the baby's emotional wavelength. It could be, however, that we notice that the mother is distracted and she misses the baby's cue. When she turns back towards the baby, she moves too far into her baby's space so that the baby stiffens. Then the mother and the baby withdraw. The baby starts to grumble: Mum picks her up and jiggles her about, but it takes time for her to settle. They have been temporarily misattuned.

Reading these perfectly ordinary interactions for their physical meaning, we are trying to understand the differing long-term physical effects on the baby of the physical/emotional event of, say, a smile offered, received, then recirculated pleasurably between the mother and baby versus the baby who finds her physical gestures mismatched. There will be no significant difference unless the mismatch predominates. All babies have times when they are welcomed and attuned to and times when Mum, or whoever is close, is not available or distracted. The issue is when the balance is in favour of mismatching. Mostly attuned-to babies will develop a confidence that their smile is enjoyed and reflected back. Their basic gesture, their basic physical/psychological self, is appreciated. Their experience is underpinned. The not-so-lucky babies, who don't experience easy matching, develop with a range of physical behaviours, from being difficult to soothe, to withdrawing and taking on a 'depressed' or withdrawn face, to developing a ready compliance and hyper-alertness to when the mother is available. We observe a mother and toddler at play and the kind of physical exchange and physical space they take up together. Is the mother able to follow the toddler's initiative, or does she perhaps inadvertently come too close one minute and absent herself the next, making the toddler's experience of the space between them precarious, so that a hesitancy and nervousness mark the space the toddler feels able to take up with his or her body?

Such physical traces are woven into both the personality

and the physicality of the baby. Faces of adults at rest can be pensive, vacant, stern, sweet, open and so on. There is a basic physiognomy which we tend to ascribe these traits to, but they are rather a combination of the physiognomy and the physical relating that the individual has experienced. You only have to look at siblings with similar facial characteristics to see the often differing emotional histories marked on their faces.

The physical aspects of our upbringing are perhaps more obvious in our grosser movements. We can look as babies begin to crawl and pull themselves up and observe how their appetite for physical development is met and then marked by their care-givers. I'm always surprised to see fathers teaching their young sons to kick. There is nothing odd in the fathers' behaviour but it is alien to me: I don't know how to kick and didn't grow up in a football family. Those little boys' muscles and their sense of joy are being associated with kicking and with Dad. When my son was eighteen months I remember the trepidation I felt as he climbed the steep stairs in our home. Seeking to control my nervousness, I reminded myself that he needed to be able to do this and that he needed to feel confident doing it. 'Go on, Lukie, you can do it. One more, sweetie. Well done.' A friend with a daughter the same age conveyed caution, as I am absolutely sure I would have done had my first child been a girl. I wouldn't have pushed myself to overcome my first-time-mother jitters.

Fashions in baby-rearing and what is to be expected of boys and girls show that there is nothing natural about the rhythms of eating, sleeping and holding to which a child becomes accustomed. Over the last century, various schemas have taken hold in the West about the proper way to treat infants. Before then, babies and children were not regarded as a discrete category of people. If you were poor you were put to work as soon as you were able, as is the case in many parts of the world today. If you were from the equivalent of the middle and upper classes, you might even find yourself living apart from your parents with a wet nurse. In England, children of prosperous families commonly lived with a nanny in the nursery at the top of the house. Mother might visit briefly each day and the children might be brought down after tea. At the age of seven, the boys would be sent off to boarding school to live in a setting in which regulation and the expectation of hardiness were enforced.

Before the age of seven, a child was treated according to the different child-rearing regimes on offer. These have swung from swaddling to demand feeding to time-tabling waking and feeding cycles. Babies born in the West in the 1950s were Truby King babies or Dr Spock babies or Brazelton babies. Today there is a contest between two principal schools of thought. There are those who, like Gina Ford and Claire Verity, believe that babies need to be trained into a sleeping and feeding routine, in which for each month of life there is a particular regime enabling the baby to feel secure while giving the parents some uninterrupted sleep themselves. On the other hand, there are those who believe that a baby's rhythm will evolve in relation to the mother's or the parents' responsiveness to his or her needs.[6] One could caricature these different approaches as parent-led or baby-responsive, but of course they are both parent-led. The parent is shaping the infant's patterns whether these are purposefully regulated or allowed to be more flexible.

Where the upfront regulators such as Gina Ford and Claire Verity come in for quite understandable criticism is in their view that crying is an expectable and acceptable aspect of settling a baby. For them, babies need reassurance about regularity. Regularity creates a sense of safety, security and confidence, and if that involves a certain amount of disciplining and wailing, so be it. For the parents who say they are following their babies' rhythms, such a practice seems cruel. They feel strongly that babies can indicate their wants. They treasure the delicate intimacy that needs to be established between parent and child. These parents also want safety and security for their baby. They believe that security emerges out of being attuned to the baby's individual rhythms rather than a one-size-fits-all set of rules applied to any child. Whichever schema is tried, however, it will imprint, like an accent, on the child's sense of self and of his or her body, patterning basic physical sensibilities for life.

The baby's sense of self is formed in the cradle of his or her developing relationships. The psychoanalyst is concerned with how the baby reacts and processes parental behaviour – not in a crude way which would suggest that if you leave babies crying then they will develop x or y symptom, but in the ways in which the developing psyche makes sense of what is conveyed and felt – especially what occurs when a baby's budding gestures are thwarted.

What is the impact when a baby's cries for food or contact are disregarded? If this is frequent, the baby will react strongly and be left with a feeling of things being not quite right. This 'not quite rightness' that the baby lives through is not trivial but stimulates psychological structures, what we psychoanalysts call defence structures, which help the baby process the 'not quite right'.[7]

The baby's mind and brain are quite literally shaped by the contact he or she receives. This works in many ways, from structuring the behaviours and feelings a baby can accommodate or reject to the development of neural connections in the brain. For example, if babies are neglected and do not experience much benign touch, benign touch will not register as a positive in their experience. Indeed, when touched in a kind way later on, they may recoil, feel frightened or anxious, because the emotional and neural pathways which code benign touch as pleasurable and soothing will not have been laid down and the experience will feel foreign and not 'naturally' benign. When it comes to a baby's brain development, a carer's ability to tune in to and talk to a baby shows up in denser neural connections than those of babies who are less engaged with. Having more neural connections aids child development. There is a significant impact. In scans developed in the 1990s it is possible to see that when babies are attuned to, similar areas light up in their brains and those of their mothers (or other attuning carers). Attunement produces security, which provides for emotional safety and what is seen and known as right-brain-to-right-brain development.[8] By contrast, misattunement on a more or less continual basis increases arousal in the brain stem, where our flight-or-fight centres are housed – the opposite of ordinary security.[9] This new work on the emotional-physical structuring of the brain is allowing us to theorise a more textured relationship between these different aspects of our development, one that pays as much attention to bodily and brain processes as it does to what has formerly been thought of as the mind. It expands our understanding of both and will provide part of the story for our being able to put together a new body–mind theory.

We've known for some time that a property of a baby's brain is flexibility.[10] What we haven't known until recently is the significance upbringing has on many different aspects of the brain, from its heating system (think of Victor surviving in the woods), to its appetitive systems, to the endocrine hormonal system – oxytocin or cortisol – that selects specific pathways based on whether the baby experiences his or her environment as generally benign and soothing or not. There are several systems that are always in play as the baby develops and the consequences of baby-responsive feeding compared to a timed feeding schema are felt at a psychological, an emotional and also a neural level.

Let's go back to one of the conceptualisations developed by psychoanalysis to explain what occurs when the baby experiences an interruption of his or her own rhythm on a consistent basis. I want to set aside the argument that rigid regularised parent-led feeding and sleeping provide their own structures of security which the baby comes to rely on and look forward to. There is obviously a truth to that, but I want instead to look at the baby for whom strict regularisation is experienced as an impingement, and see how the baby's mind and body process this experience. The baby may cry or wail, hoping to be heard and recognised. Perhaps he or she will be shushed and comforted and spoken to softly, so coming to experience that the upset can be lived through. But what if this doesn't happen? What if the baby is left to cry without being comforted, so the 'not quite right' feeling permeates his or her being? How does the baby handle that sense?

Some babies will withdraw into themselves. Some will find a way to self-soothe by sucking a thumb or banging their heads. Some will become 'easy' babies who are focused on pleasing. The outward sign dovetails with an inner psychological level. In their embryonic minds, the babies will be fathoming the sense of 'not quite right' until, and this is the tricky bit, the feel and dynamic of the parent–baby relationship become a permanent structure in their minds. The 'not quite right' and the structure that goes along with it become the babies' perception not of their situation but of their selves.

If the babies feel 'not quite right', then their self-perception becomes a problem. Babies are acutely dependent. They need responsive care-givers. The less responsive mother is to what emanates from her baby, the more the baby seeks mother's attention. The baby needs to believe, if that is the right word for the processes inside the baby's mind, that mother really is available, which means that if he or she has been left crying it must be because of some action on his or her part, some failure of his or hers. It is the baby rather than the care-giver who feels at fault or inadequate. His or her energies are then focused on reaching mother (or sibling, father or nanny). In this formulation lie the origins of a defence structure which comes into play to protect babies in their environment and keep their attachment needs viable.

For babies who develop a notion that there is something not right about them, a kind of split takes place inside their mind. A part of them stays eager and attentive to mother, while another part is watchful for what it is about themselves that will be received rather than rejected. In cueing themselves into what mother can give, the babies are structuring their psyche and specific neural pathways, which will automatically respond and put forward the parts of themselves that they sense will be received.

The innovative paediatrician and psychoanalyst D. W. Winnicott wrote about a specific aspect of the baby's personality which develops when his or her need for recognition goes unheeded. We have already seen that the baby finds the part of himself or herself that the mother appreciates. What Winnicott posits, and this is certainly borne out in the clinical situation, is that in bringing forward the parts of himself or herself that suit the mother, the baby is fitting into and developing what Winnicott terms 'a false self'. It is not false in the sense that it is inauthentic. It is false in the sense that it is an overdevelopment of certain aspects of self at the expense of other aspects, so that, in Winnicott's term, 'the true self', or as I prefer to call it, the potential self, remains undeveloped. The false self develops in response to misattunement, or what Winnicott termed 'impingement'. The mother replaces the baby's wants with desires of her own and, as the baby produces what the mother needs, the mother has the feeling that she is in tune with her baby. Her baby's creativity confirms the mother's sense of doing the right thing. But for the baby, his or her sense of security comes out of making the misattunement the emotional baseline of the relationship. This means that the baby develops certain specific behaviours and ways of being while becoming wary of what emanates from himself or herself. The baby is driven to bring forth what his or her mother is able to accept, recognise and acknowledge.

Let's see what happened with Colette, a capable, nimble, spiritually inclined thirty-eight-year-old mother of four. Colette grew up in India, the third daughter of a British colonial doctor and a French Egyptian mother. She was educated at British schools, at Cambridge and Harvard, and gave up a career as a philosophy teacher when she married her successful musician husband and started a family. Colette and her siblings had been intermittently bulimic since adolescence. Mother was particular about her food, but the family dining table in India was plentiful and enjoyable, resplendent with foods from Arabia, India and France. Colette remembers the atmosphere and the food very fondly, particularly in comparison with the privations of the British boarding school. The maids entertained the children in the kitchen and delighted in giving them special treats. Away from home and back at boarding school, Colette became bulimic after stuffing on plentiful white bread and jam for tea, and when she went to university eating and vomiting became entrenched for the next twenty years. Daily encounters with her body's insistent demand for food, and an equally persistent reflex to purge, were her most reliable and regular activities.

Colette had never felt quite right in her skin. These were the words she uttered as she explained her strict gym schedule or her dilemma on a family holiday when she would have to let go of her sarong and strip down to a swimsuit for the beach. By any kind of western cultural standard, Colette was extremely good-looking and stylish and appeared almost nonchalantly comfortable in her body in a way that might have one envying the French their style. Indeed, beside her, I felt dowdy and shabby. I'd notice minor debris on my jacket, my hair would inevitably be having a bad day: it was as though I'd forgotten how to dress. I'd scan her for hints, charmed by her aesthetic and wistful of ever attaining such savoir faire. It was an odd response. Just a session earlier I had felt physically settled, a session later too. Not that I wouldn't have minded her subtly stitched jacket or her skirt with extra flair, but I'd been free of body distress and unencumbered by disturbing body countertransferences.

She'd transferred, or I'd picked up, it seemed, a considerable and uncomfortable lack of well-being in my body. It got so that on realising it was her day to come, I would pay special attention to my clothes and shoes. I did not want to inflict on myself the internal buzzing of body disdain; I did not want to scrutinise myself as abject: it was too disconcerting. Other gorgeous women in my practice did not engender such feelings in me or send me fretting to my own wardrobe. Their physicality may have pleased me or awed me, but it was rare for me to feel that I inhabited such a disagreeable, disgruntled body myself. I knew that what I was experiencing was likely to be some complex version of Colette's own feelings about her body, the residue of what she had internalised from her mother, mixed together with my longings for her to delight in her physicality, as I did, and my own sense of myself as a woman at this moment in history, in which visual culture has cast our relations to our body as a place of hyper-criticism.

What I felt myself to be observing in Colette was the impact of a false body: a body that had adapted, that had created itself in the absence of any relation to a potential or 'true' body,[11] which because she neither possessed nor inhabited, made her bodily existence fragile. Colette's mother was a stylish woman, much concerned with her appearance in seemingly girlish ways. Today, at seventy, she still looks elegant and well groomed. She plays tennis to keep her figure trim. When Colette talks about her I see the transmission of one false body to another – a reverse Russian doll: the mother with her fragile body inside the daughter with her own fragile body. Both women learned to look great but certainly both felt very far from comfortable or content in their bodies. In the consulting room my body reverberated with the mismatching that had created such problems for Colette as she identified with her own mother's 'false' body.

We worked directly on her body difficulty. Her spiritual practices led her to daily meditations. At the gym, she would practise taking off her clothes in front of the other gym members and then walking to the shower and going to the swimming pool with just the skimpiest of towels, which she let slip before the pool's edge. She tried to allow her husband's pleasure in her body permeate her. But the embrace that I felt was required – my holding her body in my mind and my sensual/psychic taking of her body into my body, so that it could nestle in, be protected and in time experience itself as precious and adored – could not happen, because my body, now depleted of its usual capacities, felt so clipped, so useless, so incapable of offering anything of value.

After one session, as I went to write my notes, I experienced an intense burning across my skin. I felt on fire. The next session Colette recounted, for the first time, the story of her baby brother who, at the age of two, had fallen from a shelf above the stove on to the range and burned to death while in the care of his paternal grandparents and their servants. This had happened before Colette was born. I was astounded as well as sorrowful. Colette had found a way to viscerally communicate to me a bodily experience which formed an aspect of her physical sense of self.

At a conscious level, Colette's corporeal sense of her mother was of a beautiful woman who dressed magnificently. Colette would love to sit on her mother's bed in India, while long white voile curtains billowed into the room, watching her servant prepare glamorous hairdos and pampering her. Her mother would spray a little perfume on Colette and throw a scarf around her daughter's shoulders, implying that one day this glamour would be hers. Colette enjoyed this time with her mother but it belied and overlay another body sense, the burning body, which I now conjectured had also emanated from her mother and which I had picked up in my body countertransference. This burning sensation seemed to encode a sense of grief, horror, agony, shame, fear and hesitation that may have resided inside her mother's body and which she could not help but bring to the physical mothering of Colette. I imagined that I had experienced what Colette felt from her mother – the agony her mother felt about her burnt and lost child.

Colette did not talk about being touched much as a child

by her mother, although she was hugged a great deal by the maids and was a very tactile mother herself. Colette and her siblings all had eating problems and unhappy sexuality issues. The body-to-body relationship that they had internalised had been one of shame, lamentation, anguish, fear and hesitation. Unacknowledged, it precipitated down into an inert body terror which was unamenable to dispersement; it could only be passed on.

Of course I could not know, but in using the words 'shame', 'lamentation', 'anguish', 'fear' and 'hesitation' to talk about her mother's experience and the physical ambience of Colette's childhood, I was able to yank myself away from the contaminating aspects of the self-hating body countertransference I had taken on. I found myself with a body that was more receptive; in place of the dismal and second-class body I felt in so many of Colette's sessions, my body was now re-equilibrated with the far more manageable feelings of desolation, of bleakness and sorrow that were appropriate to her situation.

Working through these emotional cadences in my body and finding words to speak of bodies that were desolate, bleak and sorrowful, we began to break up the viscera of Colette's monolithically false body and to enliven it, albeit with painful feelings of sorrow and sadness. In the sequence, which of course was not a sequence but a jumble of back and forth engagements, Colette began to mourn the body she had never had: the 'free' body of childhood, the expectant body of adolescence and the delighted body of young adulthood. Encountering these imagined missing bodies was itself particularly poignant, enunciating as it did loss, longing and dismay. Now she wanted what she called her body and not her mother's. As she articulated this I began to feel less of a frump. My body was no longer primarily abject. Her comments on my footwear – my little yellow shoes or pink kitten heels – became the means by which I knew she was finding my body of some value. She wasn't walled off from it and I, richer now with my version of how I understood her pain, had a body too. It no longer felt as if she saw only its surface. It felt as if she was absorbing a body that was there for itself and for her too. My longing for Colette to have an alive body, and her ability now to feel great distress rather than be marooned in hate, had allowed her body hatred to shift.

Previous therapies, which had tried to tell her that she had transferred her self-hatred to the body, had then left her stranded with no means of dealing with this hated body. But now – via the body countertransference – she had found a compelling way for me to focus on her body as a significant experience in its own terms. We began to understand her bulimic behaviours not simply as a management of difficult feelings but as a way of swaddling a body that had no emotional myelin. The twenty-plus years of stuffing and vomiting, the frequent trips to the gym, were attempts not only to quiet and control her body, but also to make it real and stable. Winnicott tells us that a false self cannot feel alive in a continuous way. It can only find a sort of continuity and aliveness by the person creating and then surviving emergencies which in effect provide proof of their existence. And so Colette, through her bulimia, created and survived daily emergencies which temporarily reassured her of her physical existence.

Body difficulties, whether expressed as eating problems or through painful body practices, are ubiquitous in our consulting rooms.[12] This is new. I have seen this mushroom during my years in practice. It coincides with an obsessive cultural focus on the body. Everywhere we see evidence of the search for a body. Disguised as preoccupation, health concern or moral endeavour, almost everyone has a rhetoric about trying to do right by their body which reveals a concern that the body is not at all right as it is and that the body is a suitable, indeed an appropriate, focus for our malaise, aspiration and energy. We have swapped the body politic for the politics of the body, and invested our bodies with the passion and forms of thinking and engagement which suit the faction fighter in a political party. The brutality with which we judge and then treat the body reveals the desperation to make it perform as we imagine it should. Bodies in our time have become sites of display. Glamorous, virile, vigorous, sporty and healthy are our commandments, but such injunctions produce volatility and instability, making the quest unsustainable. In its place performance and enactment become desperate and often compulsive attempts at bodily recognition. We can ask whether teenagers bent on hooking up or making friendships with benefits are really as free sexually as they wish to appear. Perhaps. We can ask whether body builders downing supplements to enhance their body are simply going for strength and endurance. Perhaps. We can ask whether the teenage cutters who make ready with knives in countless girls' schools across the UK are creating a personal branding. Perhaps. We can ask whether the taking on of cyber identities in which the body is an interchangeable but essential category is just fun. I wonder. And we can question whether the multiple bodies of people who inhabit different personalities or self-states, or who are diagnosed with Dissociative Identity Disorder, are expressing bodies of choice. Certainly not. We've seen that the individual who needs his legs removed because they feel in the way is not mad. Is the individual who craves plastic surgery then simply vain? That's too easy. I think one can understand these many different manifestations of bodies rather as *crises de corps manqués*: as evidence of the desire and longing for a body; a body that can feel, a body that is touched and can be touched, a body that is stable rather than a body experiencing disorganised sensations which crave management.

It has become a feature of postmodernist thought to celebrate multiplicity, to elevate fluidity over knowing and complexity over simplicity, and to see embodiment, like femininity and masculinity, as something we achieve through performing or enacting the body we want to have.[13] In this kind of theorising, it is believed that the body can be anything we want it to be, with corporeality no more than a symbolic construct.

Playful and enriching as such ideas can be within literary theory, it is painfully apparent that they are not playful or enriching for those whose corporeal rudderlessness propels them to seek extreme solutions to what they experience as their physical incongruities. Postmodern theory is insufficient to cope with the demands of the post-industrial body. It celebrates fragmentation, a fragmentation that, in fact, requires understanding, deconstructing, nourishing and then knitting together. People whose wardrobes are so various, jangled and changeable as to engender in the observer a sense of not knowing who they are encountering from one meeting to another are not living easily in their bodies. I know from the labile bodies that I encounter in the consulting room that their 'owners' are on a search for anchoring which, once secured, perhaps allows for playfulness and masquerade to follow. But there needs to be a body there for the person in the first instance. Sam's difficulty with growing up physically is not about performance. That he has mastered. What eludes him, and many people with bodily difficulties, is the conundrum of how to have a body. The celebrating of numerous self/body states that postmodernists engage in seems to applaud the very distress of the pre-integrated body. The celebration of multiplicity unwittingly dismisses the ways in which the individual seeks a bodily coherence.

Many people come to therapy with body unhappiness. Psychotherapists are not immune to the cultural imperatives to be fit and youthful and they can understand their patients' desire, their shame and the strain placed on all of our bodies. A therapist might look at her patients and think there is little wrong with their bodies. Misguidedly she might applaud her patients' attempts at health and self-regulation, perhaps even wish for some of that very compulsiveness for herself. She might feel concern only when she sees a patient who wants to do something extreme, someone like Andrew, who wished to do away with his legs. In the United States, Argentina, Colombia and Brazil, plastic surgery in analytic patients would not cause concern, far less alarm. At an international psychoanalysis conference held in São Paolo six years ago, I was to discover how dated I was and what an oddball I appeared to be as a woman who has not been renovated from head to bottom. When patients want to have somebody operate on the labia or remove a healthy body part that is perceived to be an impediment, squeamishness may alert a therapist to a catastrophic dysmorphia considerably beyond the norm. For the most part though, psychotherapists understand and empathise with their patient's wish for a tummy tuck or unpuckered skin, or the desire for the posture, gait and health of a younger person. How could it be otherwise in a post-industrial westernised world where the body has become a series of visual images and a labour process in itself? How can the individual body possibly measure up? We manufacture our bodies. And yet isn't this also mad? The quotidian throwaway commentary on our body and its discontents expresses a culture that has been on its way to bodily disenfranchisement from industrialisation on.[14] Our tragedy is that this gross social pathology is ours to experience individually and privately.[15]

A stunted body like Sam's or one infected with colitis like Herta's or dysmorphia like Colette's raises more issues than this short book can answer. I am suggesting, in contrast with most current theory, that one should not always subsume the body self as the servant or bit player to the mind. Always situating the origins of the distress in the mind is often not an accurate or sufficient form of understanding. It is an easy kind of analysis, but it can miss the severity of the dis-ease that pertains to the body as a body. Taking on the idea of the symptomatic body as a signal of a body that is struggling to express itself and its needs, or even to exist, is more challenging and it is an important place to start.

People come to therapy when they feel broken. They don't come simply for pedagogical or intellectual interest. So when there is a question of confronting body difficulties, there should be no hesitation, no ignorance or insufficient skill in the analyst. This can only hinder work with a patient who suffers severe body hatred. It is often relatively easy to patch up someone with a body difficulty in a temporary manner. Therapists know how to do that, how to strengthen the existing defence structures so that the individual can keep on going until the next crisis. It is particularly easy to concur with a makeshift repair plan – a new exercise regimen, a new diet, a weight-lifting programme, a nutritional structure, a clothing revamp – and to see this as empowering and strengthening. We feel relieved; they feel relieved. But it is only a patch, a fudge. The aims of psychoanalysis are more ambitious than this. We endeavour to make it possible for others to be in their lives and their bodies and to feel them as generative and animated, as well as alive to ordinary discontents and longings.

4

BODIES REAL AND NOT SO REAL

Choose your first name and pick a last name from the scroll-down menu. Choose your 'avatar' – your on screen persona – but don't worry if it doesn't suit, you can modify it later. Choose a password and start to chat. Within seconds, other avatars will greet you to ask you where you are from and your age. On finding that you're too old for them, they will gently slip away and you can press a button to fly and join the other 8 million or so inhabitants, some of whom spend their days living a virtual life in Second Life, where they have set up homes and businesses.

As I type this chapter, the website housing Second Life is running in the background. I hear the clicks of people coming to greet me and check me out. I doubtless disappoint with an avatar who is a facsimile of me: a no longer young woman who is doing some research into the phenomenon of avatars and the appeal of a life lived in electronic bytes and bits rather than the forms of embodiment which have characterised life on this earth until now. I could have done what most do – pretended I was someone else, a thirty-something Spaniard who works as an architect, or a young woman getting away from her twin in Georgia. The men who greeted me and then backed away ever so kindly on finding out my age could have been my contemporaries seeking to revive some memory of their youth as they advance into late middle age and begin to reflect on mortality. Not for them the materiality of their ageing bodies. They want young flesh, even if, and maybe especially if, it is no more than a fantasy. Second Life is a space for the creation of an alternative identity. It functions as a quasi-materialised projection of desire. A poor person can 'buy' an island. The tone deaf can sing. A disabled man can garden. He can be part of what is normal. But normality is a strange concept anyway, let alone in Second Life.

The electrical impulse expressed through algorithms is foreign to me, but not to my children, for whom the computer screen is as vital to their lives as a coffee shop or the library is to mine. It's where they meet and exchange information, giving birth to identities which depend upon their imagination rather than the facts of their lives. It's not that the computer isn't compelling in my life. Whether I am writing papers, emailing colleagues, downloading articles or researching, it is all done on my laptop. There are hundreds of people I have communicated with throughout the world who are known to me only electronically. The warmth of some of the emails we exchange, and the intense back and forth that can occur when interests are shared, are exhilarating. With few formalities and little delay, almost instant intimacies are created between unknown scholars, who form a brief community of interest, then disperse as quickly as they came together.

Sometimes there are hazards. The immediacy of email and internet communication produces unexpected emotional entanglements. Like the teenager who falls for the bobble-hatted ski instructor on the slopes, only to recoil from the vaguely familiar balding forty-year-old man leering at her on the dance floor several hours later, it is easy for us to project on to a cyberspace companion intense longings and desires and a sense of being understood and responded to that we haven't felt before. People become infatuated online, not just with old loves from Friends Reunited or the hundreds and hundreds of dating sites designed to enable people to find love, but through email correspondences with colleagues they've never met face to face.

The absence of embodiment does strange things to people. It dematerialises their existence and enables the fashioning of new identities fit for the postmodern age. There is no need to be limited by the physical, the actual, the person one has been up until now. In cyberspace anyone with access to a computer terminal and the web can be an artist, creating identities, personalities and bodies that have existed until now only in one's mind's eye. Or not even. Computer technology instigates its own forms of fantasy in which we begin to create things we've never thought before. The web democratises and extends imagination, making it possible for people to enact their dreams within new communities of interest, however obscure, idiosyncratic or fleeting.

On that other ubiquitous screen, the television, sportsmen and women show their physical strengths and skills, their bodies the outcome of years of practice and training. There is nothing fictitious here; rather discipline and repetition and superb physical coordination which allow them to move deftly and strategically whether dancing on ice or passing balls via their legs or their arms. Their bodies are their product, supported by trainers, sports physiotherapists, doctors and nutritionists who aim to keep them in peak condition.

The athlete's embodiment is different in kind from the gyrating images on the music channels, whose three-minute dramas are replete with changes of clothes, attitude and special effects that convey the multiple identities a singer needs to exhibit during the passage of a song. She or he is no longer constrained by a single identity. Quite the opposite. She has to show fluidity by inhabiting many different roles: sassy working girl, dominatrix, fluffy little girl and so on. He has to show macho strength, streetwise savvy, businessman's savoir faire. The athlete's body and the singer's body stand in contrast to one another. The sportsperson's muscularity and grace derive from endless years of practice, while the singer's appearance relies on the artifice of the DVD producer, who is playing with the stylistic caprices of contemporary visual culture. The training and skill of the singer's voice are eclipsed by the promotion of her or his body in video performance.

When we move to film, the fictions about the body multiply and the apparent prowess of, say, Matt Damon and his protagonists in *The Bourne Ultimatum* is exposed. As the credits roll, we see that the fights and chases depend upon 169 stunt people and seventy special effects and digital specialists, whose agility and ability lie behind what looks like the balletic bravery of just a few people. We accept the fantastical aspects of the Bourne films: they are part of what we enjoy.

The arts have always employed artifice as a means of delighting us. Conjuring tricks enchant us because they keep us guessing. We don't quite know how the sleight of hand works or how that rabbit appears out of what, just a second ago, was an innocent flat sleeve. But we don't think about it much and we wouldn't in a film, except when we register the credits and see the multiple bodies involved in the stunts and the digital blending of those choreographed moves. Then we pause and chuckle at our ability to be captivated by the magnificent feats of Matt Damon and his adversaries.

We do not, on the whole, seek to reproduce those moves. We see them as artistry and stratagem. We know they are outside individual human capacity. The hours my children spent watching *The Karate Kid* a score of years ago were followed by personal endeavour to move as Mr Miyagi instructed. Not so today. Children turn to their supra-embodied avatars to imitate many of the tricks they've seen. Yes, they may choose one skill to perfect but they don't expect multiple talents from their own material body. They can be Spiderman and Batman in bytes. They accept this new form of inventiveness. Their energy is focused on the digital contrivances that will mirror the moves for them.

The effects of the artifice employed by the beauty and fashion industries are different. Here the space between fantasy and aspiration collapses and one melds into the desire of the other. Stylists may argue that they perform a similar kind of magic as Matt Damon's choreographers, but that is an unworthy conceit. Matt Damon's prowess is for our delectation not imitation. The industry that has created him does not require his physical reduplication. But television's numerous makeover programmes on both sides of the Atlantic – *The Swan*, *10 Years Younger*, *Extreme Makeover* – show a relentless display of the ordinary body – usually female – in the process of reconstruction. Cheekbones, teeth, noses, lips, wrinkles, lines, breasts, pecs, legs, bums, chins, feet, labias, stomachs, midriffs, hairlines, ears, necks, skin coloration, body hair become putty in the hands of the cosmetic surgeons, dentists and dermatologists, who resculpt and transform the body into its alter ego so that the end product recasts standards of what is a normal sort of beauty for all of us.

Want to look like your favourite movie star? That can be done. Want to insert a western eyelid? Join the estimated 50 per cent of Korean girls having that procedure. No problem. Have it done on the way home from school. Worried that your penis is too short or not wide enough? There are separate phalloplasty enhancement procedures to lengthen and provide girth. Been encouraged to think that post-partum labia and vaginas are an affront, or convinced that you need to revirginalise? There are surgeons to help.[1] Skin too light? There are creams or sunbeds to darken it. Skin too dark? There is a range of products, including a gene-silencer, to lighten and whiten it. Feel too short? Line up with the other Chinese who associate modernity with having a 10-centimetre rod inserted in their upper leg to put themselves on a level playing field. Feel yourself to be an over-tall Scandinavian woman? Have your upper leg broken and shortened. Breasts too large and hanging? Consider a lift and a reduction. Breasts too small? There are implants available or the newer, more 'natural' procedure of stealing the flesh from your back. Jawline sagging but uneasy about a facelift? Try a thin steel band sutured under the skin.

Surgical robotics, chemical peels, teeth whitening, hair dyeing, curling or straightening are now trivial procedures. Some techniques date back thousands of years. Decorating and reshaping the human form have always been part of our civilisation. Some cultures, have regarded circumcision, clitoridectomies or foot binding as commonplace. In others, where face markings are customary, remaining unmarked meant one was unclaimed, as though one did not have a secure place or did not belong (much like being the child of a single unwed parent in 1950s Britain or the United States).

What is new today, however, is the way in which bodily transformation is no longer linked to social ritual within the family but is part of the individual's response to wanting to produce what is an acceptable body. For those who don't have money for today's invasive surgeries or patented crèmes, ingenuity is a must. Poorer girls and women in Chinese cities are creating sticky plasters to tape on their eyelids to duplicate the look of an open, western eye. The young woman may carry several homemade eyelid openers and go to the bathroom mirror hourly to replace her makeshift 'remedy' while her male friends may stuff socks into their shoes to create extra height. It is up to each person to fix their own body as though it were in need of a redesign.

What is also new today is the extensive nature of the options. Cosmetic surgery as a consumer option is becoming normalised. The young discuss the procedures they will have. A rhetoric of empowerment[2] supports and provokes their desires and suggests that not to alter themselves would be a sign of self-neglect. Catherine Baker-Pitts's study of women and cosmetic surgery describes the quest so many women undertake in their desire to construct a different body with the help of the understanding doctor. The surgeon, both authoritative and solicitous, becomes the arbiter on female beauty. As he acknowledges the pain his patients feel, he demonstrates how he can change different aspects of their body for them enabling them to reach the beauty standard he has himself set. In his engagement with them, he gives them the body they could never imagine they would have. He is confident and persuasive. He responds to their wish with gravity but also as though they were choosing their dream holiday. In Brazil, the government meets the dream. It is willing to provide publicly funded breast enhancements to treat low self-esteem judging it to be cheaper than psychotherapeutic help. Meanwhile, holidays which combine with cosmetic surgery to Singapore, Thailand, Hungary and Colombia are promoted in western newspapers. As these practices become ever more available and widespread, people will soon ask why you haven't remodelled your body, as though it were a shameful old kitchen. Advances in cell repair and skin technology, with the use of stem cells waiting in the wings, are changing the conception of plastic surgery.[3] We are told that before long we will be going to body shops for replacement bladders, wombs, artificial retinas, brain cell transplants and so on.[4]

The earliest technologies of enhancement drew on the advances of medicine stimulated by the need to repair the severe burns suffered by many Second World War pilots. This was a very different imperative from today's demand for beauty. Wounded Air Force crews needed to be rehabilitated. Aviation fuel burned at such a high temperature that the men's injuries surpassed anything seen by medicine before and innovative experimental procedures were required to repair incinerated facial skin and ravaged noses and ears. This is when advances in plastic surgery took a leap forward.

Archibald McIndoe was the dedicated doctor who began to apply new burn treatments to the airmen. He is remembered not just as a highly skilled surgeon but as a doctor of great compassion and foresight regarding what would make the best psychological conditions for these dreadfully disfigured men going through multiple operations. An effective campaigner, he was able to get support from the Royal Air Force to build the kind of facility he wanted and to requisition a high number of 'pretty' nurses to support the men during the many operations they were to undergo. The men were encouraged to treat the hospital as a home and to wear uniforms or civilian clothes. Beer crates were stored under their beds and some men assisted at operations. To minimise the stigma from their facial reconstructions, they were taken to film premieres during wartime London and celebrated as highly respected guests.

Members of the Guinea Pig Club,[5] as these men came to be known, were battling with physical and emotional pain. They were displayed as a way of talking about the costs of war to the individual. They had flown and been shot down while serving their country. Now they were to be honoured for their valour and fortitude, not stigmatised for facial irregularity.

By contrast, today's displays of those who have undergone plastic surgery tend to be the winning contestants of TV shows. Cosmetic surgery is now something to broadcast rather than to conceal.[6] Celebrities are feted when they 'out' themselves but castigated or regarded as suspect if they choose not to showcase their new surgical assets. For ordinary women – and it's usually women – who are dysmorphic and distressed, the TV shows provide the opportunity to compete over their body distress and win the prize of radical restructuring from top to toe. To hear them tell it, they've been through their own individual wars too. We wouldn't necessarily describe their ordeal as the same as that of combatants, but their compulsion to change their bodies *is* a result of a different kind of assault on women, and increasingly men, which is sufficiently damaging to have persuaded them that the bodies they live in are urgently in need of transformation.

The cosmetic surgery industry, which is nominally medical,[7] is a growth industry. The worldwide market for cosmetic surgery and facial cosmetic rejuvenation was valued at nearly $14 billion[8] in sales for 2007 and is growing at $1 billion a year. The study 'Facial Cosmetic Surgery and Rejuvenation Markets' predicted ongoing increases in the plastic surgery market, putting the number of procedures in 2006 at well over 21 million. In Argentina, cosmetic surgery is so much an accepted part of life that it is covered in health insurance plans.[9] In addition, the worldwide market for specialised 'anti-ageing' creams and lotions, now known as cosmoceuticals to imply that they are 'scientific' preparations aimed at the disability, ageing, was estimated at over $1.58 billion in 2004 and is expected to grow at a compound annual rate of 12.6

per cent to nearly double at $2.86 billion worldwide by 2009. Market growth is accelerating as consumers in their thirties are offered over-the-counter creams and prescription products which claim to meet their needs for protective anti-ageing to repair sun damage. These preparations are warning younger and younger women, and increasingly men, that ageing starts very early. The use of models in their late thirties to advertise the products adds to this contrivance and to the suggestion that vigilance is required early on.[10]

'Start early, do often' is the chilling mantra of the cosmetic surgeons. They deploy it to expand their markets and guarantee their economic position. They have been singularly successful. The city of Tehran has 3,000 cosmetic surgeons: rhinoplasty – a nose job – is the most popular of all procedures. It costs $3,000, is performed on men and women and there are surgeons in Iran who have done 30,000 operations (or five per day) during the course of their career – more rhinoplasties than are performed by all the plastic surgeons in the UK. Plastic surgery has become a consumer item – a treat, like a holiday. I wince as I imagine any or all of the procedures now on offer. Whereas I continue to think of surgery as something best avoided unless a medical condition absolutely requires it, younger generations have a very different view. Softened up by TV programmes, they save up for it. They get excited by it. And, as Baker-Pitts shows in her studies, they see it as a right.

Sandra, a thirty-three-year-old mother of two from Brooklyn, New York, illustrates the point. She took out a loan for $10,800 for a breast reconstruction following the birth of her second baby. Like many potential cosmetic surgery patients, she would have found a brochure, 'Get the Cosmetic Procedure You Want – Today!', in her doctor's surgery, telling her that pregnancy need not mark a woman for life. Cosmetic surgery could resexualise her and erase the physical evidence of reproduction and breastfeeding. Dr D'Amico, President of the American Society of Plastic Surgeons, describes the post-pregnant body as in need of restoration, conveying a sense that the body is damaged by reproduction.[11] No wonder finance companies, accustomed to lending for cars, have found a lucrative market in lending up to a billion dollars a year to women like Sandra for surgery. Strikingly, about a third of the North Americans considering cosmetic surgery have house-hold incomes below $30,000. For some the surgery is seen as a route to economic advancement: they need a certain look to get ahead or – as it is also being marketed today – to keep a job when their spirit is young but betrayed by a sagging face. For others, cosmetic surgery is the means by which they will take part in the American dream, which has always tried to include low-income versions – whether swimming pools, cheap but fashionable clothes, bargain hamburgers, economical cars – of what is prized and valued.

While advances in burns treatment and new techniques of skin growth provide the technical base for the new cosmetic surgery, it is the photographic image – both the moving image on TV and film and the still photograph – that has created the new visual grammar. Its effects should not be underes-timated. They are changing the way we relate to our bodies. John Berger's prescient statement that (bourgeois) women watch themselves being looked at has been transmuted into women assuming the gaze of the observer, looking at them-selves from the outside and finding that they continually fail to meet the expectations our pervasive and persuasive visual culture demands.

Sixty years ago, before television became the accompa-niment to life, we were not exposed to that many images. A weekly visit to the movies presented us with glamour, risk and adventure. In comparison with today we saw relatively few billboards and magazines.[12] The painted or printed iconic images we did view were likely to be local and of a religious or political nature, relating to the values or aspirations of the community.[13]

Now there is an almost worldwide dissemination of common imagery. Globalism brings uniformity to visual culture so that what we see in London is not so different from what the billboards display in Rio, Shanghai or Accra. We are living in Marshall McLuhan's global village, sharing many of the same images worldwide. The very quantity of these images makes it impossible not to be affected by them. They become identity markers, framing our streets, our magazines, our look, providing a sense of continuity in a befuddling and fast-changing environment. We search out the brands and the signs that we know, and as we engage with these images we are not only reassured by the familiar but we make them our own, using them as a means to belong and to show our belonging. We are recognised and we recognise. This is a crucial feature of global culture, particularly for the middle class and the aspiring young. We want to belong – to be inside, not outside, the global story – and the means to enter it is often by taking up its stylistic and visually oriented markers.

It is worth considering the fact that adults can process a facial expression and match it within thirty milliseconds – without being conscious of doing so (a millisecond is so fast a human can't count it out).[14] This may be the work of the mirror neuron system, we don't know yet, but what is clear from research is that we have already taken in and responded to a look, an accompanying emotion or desire before we know we have done so. If we now apply this finding to images which are purposefully coded to be emotionally powerful by evoking mood, solution, aspiration, we realise the inevitability of our almost instantaneous reaction to the torrent of daily and hourly images around us. Many of these images are far from benign. Their purpose is invidious. They are brought to us by the merchants of body hatred.

A good 2,000 to 5,000 times a week, we receive images of bodies enhanced by digital manipulation.[15] These images convey an idea of a body which does not exist in the real world. The photo shoots which produce the raw pictures of the models are carefully lit to exaggerate features prized today and then further perfected by being Photoshopped, airbrushed and stretched. It takes a large team to create the images we see on the billboards or in the magazines or on the pop videos. There is the photographer and his or her team, the make-up artist, the stylist, the dressmaker, the fashion designer, the hairdresser. Behind them are the art directors, the account executives from the advertising side, the corporate sponsors or the magazine editors with their set of art directors, and so on. The finished product is the work of many people, mainly a skilled Photoshopping photographer and art director who stylise the image so that the finished product is far from being the outcome of a simple engagement between a pretty young woman or man whom 'the camera just loves' and a stylish photographer. In the March 2008 issue of US *Vogue*, the artistic retoucher, Pascal Dangin, changed 144 images: 107 advertisements, thirty-six fashion pictures and the cover.[16]

Photographers can now offer digital retouching on children's portraits. The gaps in the teeth or the spill of hair out of place are now proposed as flaws which can be corrected on photos rather than the capture of the unique and endearing features of the child. Children are experiencing a push to perfect their bodies at earlier and earlier ages. Where once childhood included a magical space of make-believe dreaming about how one might look as one grew, that is now disappearing. How the child appears in photos is being digitally transformed as if in preparation for the time when she will be surgically transformed. Meanwhile children are losing an accurate record of their visual history. When they look back, they will not see their own bodies but the bodies somebody else wanted them to have.

So it is too with staged photos of female celebrities, styled to reveal ever smaller waists, large breasts and ample bums on minuscule bodies, all of which infiltrate the visual field and reconstruct how we see ourselves.[17] Now we routinely judge our appearance through a hyper-critical lens, objectifying our faults. Our eyes search for uneven skin tone, less than perfectly shaped eyebrows, insufficiently plumped lips, noses too wide or too long, cheekbones too indistinct, eyes not surrounded by thick enough lashes, and so on. For each perceived defect there will be a solution, either cosmetic or surgical. This is not perceived as a hardship or oppressive but as an opportunity to improve oneself.

The beauty industry is one of the most successful 'small' global industries. Actually, at $160 billion a year, it's not so small, being a third of the size of the world's steel industry, which was worth $445 billion in 2005 and is expected to decrease slightly in 2010,[18] unlike the beauty spend, which presently has an annual growth rate which is double the GDP of the developed world (until 2007) at 7 per cent.[19] And it's expected to continue to expand.

Successful beauty companies like L'Oréal and Nivea have a growth rate of 14 per cent. They achieve this by expanding their markets to ever younger people. Girls as young as six are now playing with make-up; by eleven or twelve they may know the names of different lipstick and blusher colours from the various beauty brands and have several products in their treasure trove. Men too are being targeted (manmascara), but the most significant growth comes from those countries which are entering modernity. Cosmetics and western beauty regimens are now part of Chinese life, for example, and the use of cosmetics is seen as a way to smooth one's path towards westernisation. The 20 to 25 per cent of budgets that beauty companies spend on advertising and promotion aim to prove how imperative beauty products are.

The marketing of the beauty and style industries is ingenious. Editorial pages in magazines and style sections in newspapers name problems which hitherto didn't exist. In early 2007, a feature in one of Britain's most successful newspapers, the *Daily Mail*, focused on knees and their aesthetic challenges. Unusually the pages did not offer a treatment but nevertheless the message was clear: knees are no longer to be taken for granted. They, like every other part, require work and attention.[20]

Adroitly, or should we say craftily, the very problems the style industries diagnose are the same ones the beauty industry purports to fix. They are handmaidens in the process of deconstructing and reconstructing our bodies. And the purported fixes are offered as solutions which we can't help but wish to take advantage of. The solutions entice us. We do not see ourselves as victims of an industry bent on exploiting us. In fact we are excited to engage with and reframe the problem: there is something wrong with me that with effort – exercise, cash and vigilance – I can repair. I can make my offending body part(s) right. This psychological transaction of making a part of oneself the site of wrongness, and then pursuing perfectibility, is similar to the phenomenon I described in relation to a baby whose needs are consistently not being met by its care-giver. The same psychological mechanism is at work here. We reject the idea of being under 'assault' from the beauty industry as offensive to our intelligence. We believe that we can be critical of the negative practices of this persuasive industry and simply enjoy fashion and beauty, and yet the constant exhortation to change gets under our skin. I cited the example of the *Daily Mail* feature on knees precisely because there was no solution offered. This was so exceptional that it created a void. It stalled the baroque processes we routinely and unknowingly go through to engage with the impact images have on us. As I have suggested, we largely manage these by recasting the problem. We transform the sense of being criticised (for having inadequate lips, eyebrows, etc.) by becoming the moving and enthusiastic actor in our own self-improvement programme. We will eagerly repair what is wrong. It is as though, once having had our faults pointed out, we seize the chance to enhance ourselves by embracing the market's propositions.

In this way, the commercial interests driving the images which disturb our private body sense are hidden. When we enthusiastically embrace the cosmetic or surgical procedure, the hurt becomes less potent, as this does not appear to be an assault inflicted on us from outside but an action we desire and instigate. We see ourselves as agents not as victims. It is the individual woman who feels herself to be at fault for not matching up to the current imagery. It is not that the image is discordant. Her sightline has become faulty. She is now energised to make the new images her own signature and to express herself through these new forms. She applies herself to the job of perfecting that image for herself and so makes it her own, not assaultive or alien. Consider the impact of Agbani

Darego, the eighteen-year-old Nigerian who won the 2001 Miss Universe contest. The judges were told to pick someone who was a 'global beauty', that's to say, someone thin. And so, as Ms Darego started to appear on magazines and billboards in Nigeria she changed the aesthetic for young Nigerian women who had first experienced her look as malnourished but then went on to desire it for themselves. Inadvertently she instigated a dieting craze, a phenomena that had not previously existed in Nigeria. The language of empowerment and choice linked in with visual culture suggests to the individual woman that it is in her power to transform herself, to become the image held before her.

The beauty industry is not the only player in the war on girls' and women's bodies. It is part of the style industries as a whole of which the sine qua non is an ever more rapid change in aesthetic. Fashions to be fashionable must change. Typography, furniture, lighting, clothing, hairstyles, the phrases we use and even the cuisines we once enjoyed strike us now as quaint, ridiculous and dated. So too with bodies. We are continually updating ourselves to become a part of what is fresh and contemporary. Initially we may find the new fashions unwelcoming – stripes with flowers, wide trousers rather than tight ones – and we may feel dismay, even a certain revulsion, about the new look that is promoted, as many did with the heroin chic of the 1990s. But as similarly styled images pour out, they fill our visual field. The tight trousers that were once so much a part of who we are come to feel shabby, or inexpressive of who we feel ourselves to be or how we now want to dress. Instead of the trousers or the stripes with the flowers or the skinny heroin chic model being unwelcome, we come to feel that it is us in our own bodies, clothing and attitudes who are outdated. We become motivated to fix things so that we can feel in tune.

I don't want to cast the style industries as the big baddies. It is our own insecurities their commercial energies play upon. Undoubtedly fashions express something about the times we live in. Our current emphasis on skinniness is both an outcome of the riches the West has taken for itself and some need to exhibit, among all this abundance, its opposite: to be free of need, to be highly selective, to be able to control the food that we require, to do away with the materiality of the body. The speed at which fashion now changes tells us, however, that the pace is in large measure commercially driven. Certainly, it is hard not to see it as compulsive rather than culturally organic. Meanwhile, fashion's handmaidens in the diet, food and pharmaceutical industries play a nefarious role, adding to a sense of our bodies being a battleground.

The diet industry was estimated to be worth $100 billion in the United States in 2006.[21] For that same year, the US Department of Education budget was only slightly ahead at just over $127 billion.[22] How does the diet industry come to be worth a sum which averages out to every adult citizen spending an estimated $600 a year on diet products?[23] Since we know they aren't all spending, the amount spent by some of them must be very substantial indeed. If it is only half the adult population that spends, then the figure is closer to $1,200 a year or $3.50 a day. Not quite a cigarette habit, but a lucrative habit nevertheless for those who profit from it. NutriSystem – a diet company which successfully markets to men – increased its profits from $1 million in 2004 to $85 million in 2006. No surprise, then, that in September 2007 *Fortune* magazine named NutriSystem its fastest-growing company. Selling diets is über-profitable, but such commercial culprits can thrive only if the eating of sufficient numbers of people is chaotic. So how is it done? One factor is the segmentation of the food industry into as many categories as is possible so that we have luxury foods, healthy foods, children's snacks, ethnic foods, low-fat foods, organic foods, lunchbox treats, supermarkets' own wholesome brand, and so on. Segmentation ingeniously increases the general spend on food while playing into the idea that eating is a pastime, a consumerable with multiple choices which has as much to do with fad, fashion and emotion as it has to do with hunger and satisfaction.[24]

Another factor is the way nutritional theory lurches from one 'discovery' to another contradicting itself on the way. When I was young, steak, milk, cheese and vegetables were good. Pasta was bad. In the last twenty-five years pasta has been sometimes good and sometimes bad. White flour is indigestible, white flour is digestible. Dairy is essential, dairy is dangerous. Meat eating is good, meat eating is deleterious. Complex carbohydrates are nourishing. Complex carbohydrates irritate. Two to three glasses of red wine a day are good for the person with cardiac issues. One measure of alcohol is the maximum we should have. Vitamin A, B12, B6, zinc, etc. deficiencies are dangerous. It is easy to get too much Vitamin A, B12, B6, zinc, etc. and thus cause problems. These contradictory messages are not the ideas of cranks but disseminated in the media as the work of established doctors and nutritionists. I cite this not to create yet more confusion, but to say that nutritional developments are not so much a science as expressions of current thinking, which is often in dispute with itself and which plays into the panic about food, disturbing our ideas about when, what and how to eat. The food industry picks up on the latest press release of whatever nutritional theory or diet is around and 'aids' the consumer by designating a whole category of foods as off limits or dangerous and to be avoided. In providing low-fat (although high-sugar) substitutes, it creates a sense that ordinary processes that occur, say, in milk, such as fermentation into yoghurt or cheese, are perilous and must be altered. Fat must be taken out, although, of course, it will be sold back as an 'indulgence' in the form of 'luxury' ice creams.

The large food companies corner all ends of the market. Heinz owns WeightWatchers, Unilever owns Knorr and Slim-fast, Nestlé owns Lean Cuisine and Nespresso. The diet food market is big. And there's a reason. Start on one diet and there will always be another one to try. Diets, it turns out, promote chaotic eating. Diets can cause people to gain weight.[25] They are not a wise response to 'overweight', but are part of the destabilising of the ordinary processes of eating. So emphatically is this the case that there are girls growing up today who think that constant dieting and being frightened of food are natural states. They've seen their mothers diet and they have been initiated into that way of approaching food. Thinking one is doing a good thing for oneself, one goes on a diet. Too often the outcome bounces the girl into a pattern of dieting and then bingeing. Girls who diet are twelve times more likely to binge and develop bingeing as a way of dealing with their food.

Dieting is not a moral or a physical good. Nor are its results even neutral. Repetitive dieting disturbs the self-regulatory process which controls each individual's metabolic rate, our set point.[26] It fools the body into thinking it is responding to starvation conditions and lowers the rate at which food is processed. When people start to eat after repeated dieting, they discover that the 'thermostat' which controls their metabolism and which would normally speed up when food is plentiful has become, in a manner of speaking, stuck. Without an appropriate metabolic rate, weight gain can be disconcertingly rapid. The dismayed individual will then seek out another diet to manage the weight gain because they have designed themselves out of 'normal' eating.

There are diets for all sensibilities: no wheat, no dairy (the most common), blood groups, food combining, high glycaemic, low glycaemic, high protein, fruit diets, calorie diets, detox, feng shui and rice diets. There are diets that purport to follow a celebrity's eating plan. There are diets based on place: South Beach Diet, the Beverly Hills Diet and so on. All these regimens which curtail certain foods or food groups can be seen as ways of handling eating and body difficulties by another name. Certainly before eating problems came out of the closet, vegans and vegetarians held within their ranks many who were managing a food difficulty by excluding certain food groups. Now with dieting beginning to be frowned on, feature writers offer ways to analyse your food allergies, construct eating plans to avoid them and take supplements to enhance personal immunities. This ruse is dieting by another guise. The curious thing about dieting is that if it worked, you would only have to do it once. Diet companies rely on a 95 per cent recidivism rate: a figure that should be etched into every dieter's consciousness.[27] One wonders what forces prevent prosecution under the Trade Descriptions Act. Diet companies require return customers who will come back again and again to buy their products and services. Their profitability depends upon failure and their programmes ensure that failure happens. Likewise surgical interventions have a built-in obsolescence and in practice a guarantee of future revision or corrective work for the surgeons. Revisions and corrections are so common that some cosmetic surgery patients can purchase a ten-year warranty on breast implants.

At the pharmaceutical end of the diet industry, we find monthly articles in the newspapers about the newest medication to reduce weight. This topic is covered in the news, in the financial sections and on the lifestyle pages. Some of the cited drugs are useless or extremely dangerous for certain patients, as was the case with fen-phen, where only a minimal weight loss was achieved.[28] Nonetheless, the belief has been made current that fat equals obesity and obesity has now been reclassified as a disease that demands pharmaceutical treatment. Pharmaceutical companies with the patent on the next big anti-obesity product have become stocks worth picking. Literature that looks official and scientific, but has in fact been prepared by the public relations firms employed by the pharmaceutical companies, is placed in doctors' surgeries in the United States to extol the efficacy of this or that drug, as though a disease entity – obesity – existed that needed treating.

The West has grown terrified of obesity. To read the figures put out by the International Obesity Task Force,[29] one might believe we were in the midst of an obesity epidemic which will swamp our health service and ruin the lives of the next generation. We are told that by 2050 half of the children in the UK will be obese.[30] Without being glib and dismissing the justified concern about the growth in obesity, we need to contextualise this and see it as part of the high level of eating difficulties which beset people in the West. Many of the eating difficulties, which include compulsive eating and bulimia, are less visible than obesity but they are no less widespread; indeed, they are more prevalent.

Teenage girls in particular are so caught up in worries about their body size that very few of them eat in relation to appetite and stop when they are physically satisfied. Such concepts as appetite and satiety elude them. They are a generation who have grown up with mothers who worry about the acceptability of their bodies and who they've seen be inconsistent, wary and often anxious about their own eating, size and body shape. These daughters have learned from early on to be cautious around food, relying on rules and regulations, which they occasionally rebel against, rather than biological cues. What has become the eating norm for teenage girls is far from what would have been considered 'normal' eating twenty years ago. Playing about with appetite, or eating only on weekends, or just one meal a day, or some such scheme, can indeed lead to thinness, but because it cannot be sustained, it can equally well lead to fatness. Emotional and biological rebellions against a life of food restriction, deprivation and compulsive exercising can produce either anorectic-style responses or what appears to be its opposite – out-of-control eating.

From the therapist's point of view, these two forms of managing food share complementary characteristics. Anorectics have a tendency to overestimate their size. The obese tend to underestimate theirs. Neither see themselves as they are. Nor do either have an easy time accepting their appetites. The people whose eating difficulty expresses itself in an anorectic manner are so afraid of appetite and desire that they create a situation in which they are indeed hungry, they experience it, but their hunger is there to reassure them that they can do without nourishment, that they do not require much. Their emotional and physical appetites feel unwieldy and wrong unless they are overridden. In controlling their hunger and what emanates from them, they are showing us a food-oriented version of a response to a false body.[31]

People who eat in an out-of-control fashion also find hunger and need intolerable: they cannot bear to experience their need. Their response to the dilemma of appetite and desire is to eat in advance of feeling what for them is too painful a call of hunger.[32] It is possible to understand this prophylactic eating as another version of the false-body phenomenon. Whether striving for thinness, afraid of it or managing it, a fear of appetite and an unreliable body sense stalk many girls' and women's days. Thinness has become an aspirational issue, a means to enter what on the surface appears to be a new class-less society. But it is – falsely, I believe – promoted as a health issue in which the psychological underpinnings of appetite and thinness are bypassed. Often behind the desire for thinness – which affects those who are fat, those who are thin and all sizes in between – there exists an unhappy, unhealthy relationship to food and to the body. When confusions are created around size, when size depends on the transformation of personal biology and not on knowing and responding to when one is hungry and when one is satisfied, there can be no peace. The sense of having a stable body whose size and appetites one knows and can trust is elusive.

The recent emphasis on the Body Mass Index (BMI) compounds the problem. Interestingly, few medical people who are actually working in the area of nutrition and obesity find it a useful measure. There are better predictors for heart disease and diabetes which depend on the girth around the midriff area rather than the BMI, which is itself a crude measure of the ratio between height and weight. It was devised by the Flemish scientist Adolphe Quetelet in the mid-nineteenth century when the infatuation with social Darwinism made statistical measures all the rage.[33] In 1995 the World Health Organisation, under pressure from the International Obesity Task Force, revised the BMI in such a way that 300,000 Americans who had previously thought they were 'normal' weight woke up to find themselves reclassified. Brad Pitt and George Bush, for example, were now overweight (a UK example would be Linford Christie), and George Clooney and Russell Crowe were obese. I think we can see how preposterous these classifications are and thus question the estimates categorising 50 per cent of our children in danger of becoming obese. We can also question who is helped by this reclassification and examine the deleterious effect it has on our relationship to our bodies,[34] especially if we look back to the 1950s, when ads proclaiming 'Skinny? You'll miss out on summer fun!' sold 'super wate-on' tablets to help women 'put on pounds and inches of healthy flesh' to encourage that era's aesthetic, which was certainly a BMI in the 27-plus category.

In collapsing a multitude of eating problems into the newly minted disease of obesity, we see the legitimating of commercial enterprises that swell their profits by creating panic around size and shape. Despite the newspaper column inches and the television documentaries about the obesity epidemic, there are few sustainable facts here. The studies claiming that 365,000 people a year in the US will die from obesity, that one in three children are obese and that a BMI of under 25 is optimum have all been shown to be fanciful. In fact on the National Institute of Health's reanalysis of its own figures, one in fifteen children are seriously overweight in the US and some 26,000 will die from obesity-related diseases. Contrast this with the US figures for smoking-related deaths per annum of 600,000.[35]

Obesity is a problem. I don't want to underestimate it. But I want to be sure that we see the social, psychological, class, visual, nutritional and commercial issues behind the so-called crisis. People may be eating more than their bodies require, their bodies may not be processing their food well, they may be eating foods which are hard to metabolise. This is certainly one part of the body story.[36] So, too, is the aspirational thin-body story emerging in the new economies of eastern Europe, Arabia and Asia. Then, too, the fat body may be refusing our visual and aspirational culture, saying, 'I don't want this. I can't manage this,' or telling a story of the unhappiness which is encased in the fat body. The fat body could be challenging our overpowering preoccupation with image. It might signal a dismissal of childhood eating regimens. Or it might be more a statement about consumerism and the impossibility of so-called 'choice'.

If we recognise how ways of eating can indicate a crisis around the body, it is possible to see that fatness is as much – if not more than – an indictment of our culture, as it is a site of individual 'failure'. Given that obesity is now being linked to poverty and low income, we also need to take note of class issues and how aspiration plays out for many who experience economic exclusion. And of course more complex thought is required to supplant the oversimplistic talk of calories in and calories out which dominates government thinking. We need to insist on the links between the rise of obesity and the intensification of visual images of thin people; the introduction of long shelf-life foods saturated with fats, soy and corn syrup; the extraordinary growth of the diet industry; and the segmentation practised by the food industry, who take out fat from one food, such as milk, and sell it back to us in another. These four events parallel the rise of obesity. You could produce a graph showing the rise in the sale of low-fat milk and another that showed rising obesity numbers and they would fit perfectly. Similarly a graph of the growth of the diet industry would fit with one showing the rising numbers of larger people. And it is also the case that the rise in obesity statistics coincides with our increasingly sedentary lives and the preponderance of images of the incredibly lean.

Health economists and city planners are hard at work discussing the impact of the car and the design of our towns, shopping centres, rural transport and lighting in order to encourage us to move our bodies and eat sensibly as a matter of course. That is very important. But this focus can miss out on the emotional, psychological and class meanings attached not only to food and eating but to size. In an image-based culture, the conscious and unconscious meanings of fat and thin are highly complex. While fatness might be regarded as laziness and indulgence, this is far from the experience of the eater with bulk.[37]

The designation of fat as worthy of scorn and dislike, and of fat people as outsiders who should not only dislike themselves but also be discriminated against, is growing. This is not a new phenomenon (hence the organisations that exist to defend the rights of fat people) but the disrespect has intensified.[38] Fat and fatness are now demonised and are seen as signals of class. Yes, there are class issues involved in food distribution, food costs and nutritional education, but the contempt with which people now talk about fat and fat people indicates something else. This is now viewed as a condition to be avoided, since it signifies both a loss of psychological control and membership of the wrong class, with an implied set of false aspirations.

There is some discussion now about whether the diseases which are becoming more prevalent, such as diabetes, actually cause obesity or are caused by it.[39] Some are suggesting that the content of food (such as high concentrations of corn syrup) can produce diabetic responses. There is also clear evidence that the most protective weight for health purposes is a BMI of 27.5 (if one accepts the BMI at all) – a figure that is presently in the recently designated overweight category. Interestingly, overweight people who exercise have a lower mortality rate than thin people who do not. So one is led to wonder why thin has erroneously become the gold standard for health. Could it be that even though the evidence does not support the idea of thinness as healthy and good, the overwhelming power of today's visual aesthetic has affected even doctors and medical researchers? The social phenomenon of fads and scares has been well explored. The so-called obesity epidemic is one of them.[40]

There is extremely disturbing evidence that one contributor to actual obesity is low maternal weight – the goal of so many women today. How many women are encouraged to feel proud that they don't show until the sixth month of pregnancy? Yet there may be a hidden danger in promoting low weight in pregnancy. At the end of the Second World War, the Dutch suffered an extraordinary famine. Women who were exposed to the famine in the first six months of their pregnancies had underweight children who became obese as adults. Those experiencing starvation for the first time in the last trimester did not. Epidemiologists reviewing these results are now beginning to think that low maternal weight in the first six months of pregnancy primes a baby to act as a famine victim and that low-weight babies are more likely to become diabetic. If we combine this information with the recent trend for celebrity mothers (and hence other mothers too) to have elective Caesareans before term because of the perceived advantage this will provide in the rapid recovery of a trim post-pregnancy body, we see how an emphasis on thinness – 'pregnorexia' – can be a risk to both mothers and babies. The impact of the war on women's bodies has been to create tension in the very earliest weeks of a baby's life as physical holding and bonding are impaired, affecting both the mother and the next generation.

The numerous industries – diet, food, style, cosmetic surgery, pharmaceutical and media – that represent bodies as being about performance, fabrication and display make us think that our bodies are sites for (re)construction and improvement. Collectively, they leave us with a sense that our bodies' capacities are limited only by our purse and determination. In another part of the woods, mainly in the academy, the transhumanists dream of a not so distant time when the actual capability of the human body will be so extended that we will be able to do things that we associate now with futuristic movie fantasies. For them, technological enhancements for the human being have no imaginative limit. They believe that the body can be re-engineered to such an extent that death, unless caused by homicide or an accident, will have become a bygone biological process.

What interests me is the thrust of the dream. Bodies do have limits. Life is what happens between birth and death. The human condition inclines us to extend the limits we find in life and strive and strain against them in the knowledge that they nevertheless exist. For some bio-ethicists, the limits are viewed as a challenge.[41] Mind is all. Body is for augmentation. Enhancing cognitive and physical capacities makes us more than human, hence the term transhuman. The transhumanists argue that because 25 per cent of the population of the US already have some kind of bodily implant – whether removable, like contact lenses, or permanent, like pacemakers, stents or tooth implants – the jump to tiny embedded personal computers will be commonplace. These might provide us with foreign vocabularies, the skills to carry out complex physical tasks such as robotics do now, and transform our bodies in ways which are currently unthinkable. Children will grow up with technological enhancements available to them just as we have become accustomed to microwaves, mobile telephones, computers and gene splicing. For transhumanists the idea of a fixed or limited body is an anathema. They hold a hyper-Descartian view. It can be characterised as 'I am what I think and what I can leverage – via new technology – my brain to do.'[42]

The enhanced human body, the so-called transhuman body, speaks to my psychoanalytic mind as a search by the wounded, decontextualised body to find some relief by decorporealising itself so that the physical body experiences no restriction, no boundary, no ordinary human frailty. It is the body as supremely dematerialised and ironically disembodied. A body that tires, that hurts, that decays, that is exuberant, that is joyful, that stumbles and pauses, is erased. In its place is a cyberised body directed by the fantasies the mind and the engineers can invent.

Certainly, we need to keep abreast of what insertions and enhancements are planned and where the ethical boundaries lie. As we age, we may come to rely more on prosthetic devices and hope that drugs will be developed to stop loss of memory. But this is very different from longing for a transhuman body, a longing which underlines how unstable and dismal our relation to our body can be today. The body has become a casing for fantasy rather than a place from which to live. It is not Luddism on my part to suggest that in a world mad in its relationship to the body, the solution lies not in fleeing from the body's materiality but in engaging with the difficulties that our bodies present to us at a psychological, personal and social level.

As I read about transhumanism and allied endeavours such as the current research to get pharmaceutical chemicals to wipe out emotionally traumatic memories so that we will be able to do away with pain-filled histories, I wonder what kind of electronic implant can effectively override the pain messages to the brain. Pain is a signalling system. It warns us of danger. Knowledge of the pain we are in is part of the experience of being human. In general we respond by avoiding the painful stimulus as best we can. We get our fingers burned and we learn not to put them in the fire again. But a good deal of pain is not a simple conditioned response. Pain is also a human idiom, and when individuals use pain as a desperate appeal to enunciate despair about their body, we learn something not just about their body – as in Colette's or Herta's – but about bodies in our time. If we think of the many people who engage in self-harm or are drawn to the kind of rigorous exercise that causes pain, we cannot look at pain as simply a disturbance in the brain cells. Pain has meaning; many different meanings. Pain – psychological or physical – alerts individuals to reflect on their experience. Pain may be the way they find of enacting the contamination from a culture that attacks the body physically or mentally. We have tended to respect physical pain and disparage mental pain. But the situation is not quite so simple. The distinction between the two is less mechanical than we believe. The mind affects the body and the body affects the mind in a complex loop. What, where and how one experiences physical pain and the way it affects one has much to do with personal circumstances as well as the medico-physical events that are occurring. We all know people who are able to 'suffer in silence' or perhaps appear not to suffer physically, and we know others for whom pain is their salient experience. What interests me is that psychosomatic pain was always judged to be about the mind's tricks on the body, while my psychoanalytic experience has taught me to take notice of the physical, corporeal aspects of my patients who are in physical pain because their pain is not only about their minds but also about their attempts to find a body for themselves. In being in the kind of physical pain and distress that requires attention, they are trying, I believe, to bring an attentiveness to a body that has been neglected, disregarded or mistreated. It is private and personal and their amplified pain is a mechanism of self-communication and self-expression.

Of course, those who work in pain management quite properly want to bring relief to those who suffer unbearably. Chronic pain is debilitating. The effort to find drugs to neutralise the pain are comprehensible and laudable. It is the transhumanists' wish to do away with pain that is a curiosity, as it seems to deny – along with so much else – the ordinary experience of being human.

If we turn the emphasis from those who wish to heal towards those whose aim it is to hurt and look at torture for a moment, we see that in torture we cannot lose the actuality of the body. Pain is torture's intent. The impact of torture gains its potency from its ability to inflict unbearable physical and thus psychological torment on its victims. The body as body is inescapable; it is torture's first domain. Torture depends upon acts of extreme and calculated violence. It intends to threaten, destabilise and pervert the beliefs and intentions of the individual. Torture is designed not only to reveal what the tortured person wishes to hide but also to subvert the mind of the individual so they distrust themselves. It is designed to show that the master of the body is not its inhabitant but its torturer.

Very few can withstand physical torture. The mind can separate out what is happening to it for short periods of time by dissociating, but it is an adage of those who engage in acts for which they may be tortured that their companions should assume that what information they hold will be prised from them. The aim of torture is to steal the integrity of the individual: to separate mind and body in such a way that the mind is destabilised. The body too, as its physical functions become involuntary under the pressure of sleep deprivation, disorientation as in waterboarding, and physical assault. What has been interesting in the *Big Brother* reality-TV approach taken by the perpetrators of the Abu Ghraib tortures, documenting their own excursions into body cruelty, is the filming of their sadistic endeavours. Two things come together here about modern life. Reality-TV shows situate the audience as spectator and witness to the indignity of others failing at a difficult physical challenge, not being able to withstand the fear of being in a jungle, or of being voted off a show. A taste for voyeurism is developed. This then joins with the visual capture of the humiliations. On our screens we see people shamed and put down.[43] As audience, we are participants in their ignominy. If we now add viewing political torture to the mix, we can reflect on the phenomenon that torture has always been documented. There are extensive Nazi records of torture, just as there are in Phnom-Penh. The recording of torture per se is not novel. It is the visual documentation of torture as home movie that suggests something quite desperate about our relation to the body. We see the body being violated. We see appalling acts of aggression visited on detainees. We become bystanders to physical and emotional abuse. The filming makes real how bodies at war can perform aggression on other bodies. In the videos, the physical enunciations of assaults on our bodies, which usually go unseen, are exposed. The horror of that form of physical engagement is made real. A sadism bent on evisceration is exposed and we are left wondering whether the torturers – and ourselves as watchers of the videos – may also be seeking to experience, by proxy, an intensely physical cruelty which tests the limits of the human mind and body. The culture's perpetual investigation of bodies is now revealed in the full horror of torture. Viewing torture becomes the manifestation of a culturally perverse relation to the body. This affects us all.

Since the 1970s and more explicitly in the 1990s, the French artist Orlan has used her body as a canvas on which she inflicts physical cruelty. She submits herself to the cosmetic surgeon's scalpel to be carved and reshaped. She confronts us with the horror of the procedures, with the intensity of the desire for change, with the impossibility of having a body that one can find acceptable. Her work is almost too painful to look at. This is the point. She directs us to see what we would rather not acknowledge: the pain and the destructiveness which devolve upon the female form. We weep when we force ourselves to absorb what she has put herself through, as she enacts in exaggerated form what women are encouraged to do to their bodies.

The assault to which Orlan voluntarily subjects herself is an attempt to make art out of the assault inflicted on women all over the world. As we saw earlier, cosmetic surgery is not art for many people today but emotional survival. In some cases, particularly in China, South Korea and the new countries of eastern Europe, cosmetic surgery is perceived to be a question of economic survival: a way of ensuring 'a level playing field' or a passport to higher earnings. The power of the magnified and manipulated photographic image has left us with the sense that to attain the right kind of bodies, most of us have to fashion and fix what we have. Orlan makes the tragedy of that search explicit and she disabuses us of the idea of empowerment which accompanies the many body transformations on offer today. Like the filmed torture, she shows us how destabilised bodies have become in that we can consider plastic surgery as a place of joy and celebration. She shows us how distress is the body's calling card.

With the body judged externally, dismay will be rife. Success means looking younger every year, as the women in the gym seem to. Success means regulating the body: controlling hungers, desires, ageing and emissions. Success means seeing the body as a lifelong work. Success means anticipating faults – physical, medical and aesthetic – and correcting them. But when and if the ordinary processes of the body cannot be sufficiently restrained, which of course they can't, the body becomes a source of consternation as well as failure.

The paradox of wishing to be free of unruly and inconvenient bodily demands so that one might live peaceably from within one's body is intensified. The body is experienced as menace. From this perspective, we cannot but fail. Our bodies are bound to be wrong. It is not our stance towards the body that is seen as problematic. There is no space for such a shared critique. Instead, we feel that the problem lies in the ineptitude of our individual endeavours. We have failed to create the body as it should be or how we want it to be. We have only a temporary peace, with the next opportunity to take 'it' in hand and attempt to keep refashioning it medically, emotionally and physically around the corner. There is no such thing as a body that can simply be.

5

AND SO TO SEX

The school-bus drivers of middle school children in the Philadelphia suburbs were getting upset. On both their 8 a.m. and 3 p.m. runs they had noticed that the heads of several young girls were bobbing up and down on boys' laps in the unmistakable rhythm of oral sex. These girls between the ages of eleven and fourteen who still needed to be driven to and from school somehow perceived that grown-upness meant sexually servicing boys. The bus drivers spoke to the school authorities, who simultaneously learned that several boys had come to the offices of student counsellors feeling shamed and bewildered when the girls initiated oral sex.[1] Both sexes were confused. It's hard for the young to understand their place in the sexualised world they have inherited. In this case, it was also hard on the bus drivers, though easy enough for them to respond moralistically. The mismatched sexual exploration they witnessed isn't exactly what the post-Freudian sexual revolution had in mind. Sex was meant to be expressive and joyful; not obligation for the girls and embarrassment for the boys.

On www.hotornot.com, a mainly teen website on which girls and boys put up a photo of themselves, 12 billion votes have been cast on a scale which rates them from 1 to 10. Nothing here but the pictorial; the very best photo a girl or boy can muster.[2] In this age of the highly manipulated visual, ordinary girls and boys are trying their luck through touting their bodies on screen. They learn to light themselves in a flattering manner, stand like a model, pout like a movie star and show their washboard stomachs. It's quite democratic really.

A relatively cheap technology, available in schools, community centres, internet cafés if not at home, allows 'everyone' to partake of Andy Warhol's notion that we will all have fifteen minutes of fame. Whether in Belgrade, Denver, Shanghai, Cusco or Moputu, we have the ability to have our own pages on Facebook and YouTube, to compete for visual space on sites such as hotornot.com or facethejury.com or become a contestant in the increasing number of spin-offs from *The Swan*, *10 Years Younger* and *Extreme Makeover*.

What these sites tell us is that, as far as sexuality goes, the body is all. But while it is the currency for girls and boys to display, their bodies also have to be judged and rated. The competition makes explicit that this is a search for recognition through sexual attractiveness, not dissimilar to the recognition the girls fellating the boys are seeking. It is a recognition they mostly fail to get because what they are looking for resides neither on the websites nor with the boys' as yet immature penises and emotional capacities. The girls want to be seen, to pass the threshold of physical attraction, to know that they are special and individual, while existing as part of a peer group. But the boys can't quite recognise them sexually or emotionally. They are too young.

Of course girls don't only seek this recognition from boys. They seek it from girls. As a gaggle of girls make their Saturday night preparations in front of the mirror they advise one another on outfits, hair, make-up, shoes, bags, jewellery, perfume: the external accoutrements of femininity. They are making personal the exigencies of visual culture. With energy and excitement they enlist one another to overcome the insecurities that have been imprinted on their body sense, whether these have come primarily from their mothers, as in Colette's case, or through cultural image saturation. They savour creating a fashionable look while being idiosyncratic and personal. Theirs is an often joyful engagement, not one that they would describe as oppressive. They are trying to make a body that feels attractive and they relish the process. No wonder. They aren't isolated in their own bedrooms dealing with their private dismays. They have one another to help them emphasise their good points and provide hints to minimise what they don't like. It's a new world for girls in which beauty, as we have seen, and sexuality become important early on. But something is missing. They don't really have a sexuality for themselves any more than they have bodies which feel stable. They know sex is important but what it is, where it comes from and what it is for, elude them. That lack of knowing is what makes it possible for them to think that sucking off young boys on their way to school will help them. But it doesn't. So they veer towards that other imperative: being attractive. They enlist their girlfriends, who are in a similar position, to help them create the look that says 'sexy'. Later that night, or in a few years' time, some of these girls will binge-drink, end up having sex and posting their before and after pictures on Facebook. They need to be seen.

Age compression, the phenomenon by which girls are expected to dress and behave older than their years, is accelerating. Now there are stilettos for babies (with collapsible rubber heels) and bra sets for toddlers. No wonder issues of age and sexual readiness become problems for American pre-teens and teenagers.[3] They are scanned and evaluated as they endeavour to make the grade as 'hot'. It's a tough call. And while it starts young, it goes on and on. Britney Spears is only the latest woman to attract condemnation for the affront of daring to dance in her post-pregnancy body. A body once admired for its polish and sexuality is now damned for the consequences of the sexual act that produces babies. The disconnection between the sexually attractive body and the chaste body that seems to accompany our view of procreation is a paradox we have long lived with. The mother has been presented as a desexualised Madonna who, until the mid-1980s, was expected to wear demure clothes to disguise the very sexuality that produced the pregnancy.[4]

This upside-down notion of the sexual body remade as pure is only one of the complex and clashing ideas we live with. Consider for a moment the external body judged as a sexual surface. The visual predominates. Sexual desire comes from seeing. The emotional, spiritual or committed connection which has underpinned Judaeo-Christian morality around sex is evaporating. It is not just that attraction is physical, for in some ways it was ever thus, but that physical attraction is sanctioned as the basis for action, for sexual encounter. In the last forty years, as we have dismantled the rule book about sexual morality, about who it is all right to sleep with, and when and why, desire has been 'freed' and a compunction to act has replaced the compunction to desist. Attraction is all. Meanwhile in those cultures and religions in which women are expected to conceal their bodies or take part in arranged marriages, it is still very much the visual, the way a woman's body looks, that is considered inflammatory.

Today's visual muzak crashes into the old taboos about the visibility of the female form, putting a new spin on the age-old idea that the female body is dangerous: dangerous to women and dangerous to men. The female body has been considered to be so sexually powerful that it can overwhelm. It must be hidden. This past power of women's sexuality contrasts in one way with the dilemmas of today's young women, who don't trust and don't know that their bodies are powerfully attractive just as they are. They feel they must work hard to get their bodies to be sexually alluring. But then in a reprise of the experience of many women, whether they have been encouraged to hide their bodies behind veils and long skirts, or cut their hair and wear wigs, or dress up like a celebrity, the premium on the body produces often unrealisable erotic dreams which may go unfulfilled because the confirmation of sexuality and body acceptance they seek cannot then be met. The pre-formulated view of female sexuality carried both by girls and women and by their boyfriends and partners – male or female – can preclude it.

The sexual today has been hyper-stimulated. The use of sexualised bodies to represent and sell us the good-life story of consumer society provides us with pictorials of how we should present ourselves as sexual beings and how we should look while we are engaged in sex. *Zoo* magazine has recently run a competition in which men send in pictures of their girlfriend's breasts and the breasts of the celebrity they most desire. The winner's prize is to have his girlfriend's breasts remade to resemble those he longs for.[5] No wonder sex is something women watch themselves doing with a third eye. The moves they make, the gestures of flirting and even of sexual intimacy, are exciting because they reference images from movies, TV and music videos. Sex becomes an act which, by being performed, confers on the participants a sense of the erotic. Whether it is erotic in and of itself is something I am not so sure of. Certainly in the case of Ruby – whom we shall soon meet – and many of the women I have seen in therapy, sexuality has to be conjured up and becomes a performance. It doesn't exist or flow organically. A combination of the notion of the visual and the legacy of the mother–daughter relationship, in which a mother's job has, until recently, been to proscribe rather than encourage sexuality and the erotic, has made sexuality a 'thing' to purvey and display as a personal body stamp. While sexual mores have been much in flux of late, a mother's attitudes towards her own sexuality and the proscriptions she herself experienced in her upbringing will be part of the mix of attitudes a daughter absorbs as she tries to enter into a meaningful erotic for herself. For girls and women (and for some young men in metro-sexual and gay male culture too) sexuality may be experienced as an essential add-on – something they conjure or create for a purpose rather than experience as an integrated and organically expressive aspect of self. As the wider culture becomes more and more compulsively sexualised, so the individual can experience a clash between sex as the commodity one brings to the world or a relationship, sex as a place of confusion and disappointment, and sex as an expression of intimacy.[6]

A British Sunday newspaper recently invited its male readers to send in pictures of their girlfriends. The winner would be offered a session with a porn star to learn how to turn her man on. It's no surprise that lessons in seduction, showing a woman how to feign lack of interest on the one hand and gyrate around a pole on the other, are widely taken up. That these classes appeal to women from their twenties to their fifties is interesting. Like the teenagers getting ready on a Saturday night, these women experience their sexuality as not quite integrated. It is rather something that requires lessons or preparation. The visual objectification of sexuality and the phenomenon of sex as a personal asset or commodity have freighted the body, or perhaps I should say the idea of the body, in ways that can feel unsustainable. The body must signal sexuality. The sexual can have any number of guises, from innocent schoolgirl look to sadistic school matron, but signal it must. The sexual body must be able to make moves from purring seductions to sinuous gymnastics. The often unrealised instructions we carry in our head direct one to be sexual in preordained ways. Unsurprisingly, then, when an insecure and unstable body engages in sex only in ways that have to do with look and performance, an individual's sexuality is measured (by that individual as well as by the other) by the extent to which one's representation meets the current markers of sexuality. The ideal of a sustainable body capable of enjoying sexuality and sharing vulnerability can be elusive.

Of course this stress on how the body looks is not confined to girls and women. On dogging websites, which have become popular in the UK over the last five years, people exchange information prior to arranging to meet for sexual purposes. The specificity of bodily requirements displayed and asked for is astounding. A man shows a picture of his washboard stomach – no head, no face, no legs or arms, just his torso. A homosexual site asks one to tick boxes to describe oneself and one's physical requirements: moderately hairy chest, very hairy chest, waxed chest, and so on. The sexual becomes an encounter with a body image.

At the same time, the longing for and pursuit of sex have become compelling activities for many people, precisely because the sensations they engender are intense and remind us that we can be excited, touched and moved rather than simply experiencing our body as a performance. Like feeling the pleasure of physical exertion, sexual sensations can bring authenticity to our bodily responses even if they are unable to produce a body sense that feels reliable and stable for the individual. In making this point, I am highlighting a somewhat tricky paradox. Sex is, as we know and appreciate, a potentially powerful meeting of bodies. It is also the place where people can be sufficiently vulnerable and open and find the confirmation that they and their body are all right, acceptable, beautiful and alive. We seek it in sexuality precisely because the erotic, with its physical power, can cross the feelings of inauthenticity – both physical and emotional – which beset so many people today.

Psychoanalysis started with sex. In exploring the discontents of the Victorian bourgeoisie, Freud gave us a story of human nature and our place in the world which is motivated by sexual repression and conflict. In his account, female sexuality was a poor substitute for male sexuality. Its development required from the young woman the tortuous task of turning away from a girlhood of being active and pleasure-seeking into a passively receptive womanhood – a configuration in which the woman was prepared to receive the active sexuality of masculinity. Freud was effectively pinpointing what he had observed about the hesitations of female sexuality. He wrote about what he saw and he posited this process of active turning into passive as a way of understanding the position of women and of women's erotic at the time.

Freud's ideas emerged at the same moment as the first feminist wave, in the late nineteenth century, and there was some doubt whether he would survive twentieth-century feminism.[7] Lambasted as a patriarch, he and his work would have been jettisoned but for two aspects of the liberation struggles of the 1960s and 1970s which saw his value. First, when sexual liberation became one of the aims of the various movements, there was a need for a theory sufficiently cognisant of unconscious processes and sexual relations. Secondly, we needed a less mechanical theory than the economic ones which attempted to explain – and did to some extent – women's own participation in their subordination and the construction of a feminine psychology. Psychoanalysis seemed a productive way to address these questions; but we had to get over the hump of whether Freud was correct in his view that women needed to move from being active to passive, and if so how this occurred? We did it by reading Freud's account of the sexual and gendered ordering of society as a description of what existed rather than what should exist. His work and methods could then be excavated for how we become psychologically gendered people.[8]

If we reflect on the changing sexual climate today, we find that Freud's methodology of putting together behaviour with unconscious desire and conflict is extremely useful. His approach opens up questions that enable us to see the discomfort and concern of the bus drivers and school counsellors in relation to the eleven- to fourteen-year-olds mentioned at the start of this chapter. A psychoanalytic approach suggests that contradictions are driving the girls' early sexual activities. The blowjob is performed to reassure the girls. The driven nature of their bestowing of unwanted sexual favours exposes the girls' insecurities. They are desperate to do something sexual so that they can feel they have mastered 'it', as though 'it' were an accomplishment. They are being active. But this activity is in pursuit of a self-worth which they can garner by enacting something. It is not sexual expression. Their belief that they have to do 'it' shows us that pre-teen femininity is in trouble and that sex on the surface may not be about sex in the unconscious. Their acts express the sexual confusions and conundrums of late modernity in which sex is for show. They may also in part be a consequence of the way in which sexual hygiene is featured on a school curriculum: in sex education classes girls learn how to put a condom on a partner rather than how to locate and relish their own sexual pleasures. In a reversal of how popular culture understands the Freudian formulation, psychoanalysis suggests that the girls' fellating activities may not be sexual. They may be searching for connection or a way to enunciate just how difficult and confusing sexuality and the body are for adolescent and pre-adolescent girls.[9]

Are these the girls, one can speculate, who then go on to cut and harm themselves? Who, failing to get the contact they need from the young boys, find their wish to be valued so roundly misunderstood (and thus rejected) that they harm themselves for having desire? An old-fashioned Freudian would be inclined to view a person who cuts their body as responding to unresolved sexual dilemmas. The phenomenon of cutting was not that widespread until twenty years ago and an off-the-shelf Oedipal explanation was seen to suffice. But today, with the explosion of cutting behaviour, I think we need a more open approach. Yes, cutting oneself might be sexual in origin,[10] but equally it could be a way of enacting a violence that the woman or girl has experienced. Self-inflicted cuts may be a search to show to oneself and others emotional pain that is initially felt to be outside language, while at the same time revealing how unstable the body as a body is.

Jane's story reflected all the aspects of cutting. She was a thirty-year-old from Ohio. Her background was religious and we had reason to believe that there may have been sexual abuse in the family. A seamstress who worked with a needle, Jane sliced so deeply into her breast with a knife every four months or so that she bled copiously and required sutures and immediate emergency room treatment. She didn't hear voices which told her to cut herself. She described her body as a jangle of painful sensations and her mind as intermittently flooded with feelings of unreality. Then her eyes would stare, she said, looking at the world through blackened gauze. When she started to talk about the need to cut, painful contradictions emerged. She lived so much in a sore and unhappy mind that she felt she barely existed in a material sense. Her body was unimportant to her – it was unkempt. Her cutting behaviour was partially done in order to help her feel and find a body self. When she made herself bleed spectacularly, she was faced with the physical reality of her being. The cutting enabled her to engage with what she tried to ignore – her body. She now had to care for it and notice that it was where she lived. Her assault on it paradoxically brought her body self to life, while temporarily quieting the chaos in her mind.

It helped that the cutting caused a chemical reaction – a surge in cortisol, which in its wake brought a cascade of epinephrine to soften the pain invading her. At the same time, it made visible and visceral, to her and to those who knew or saw what she had done, the horror of her mental and physical pain. Sex did this for her too. Not the close sex of a loving relationship or the ephemeral warmth of an encounter with a stranger. The sex that calmed Jane had overtones of violence and danger. It required an anonymous encounter in which some fantasy or actuality of violence occurred. She needed physical hurt to feel soothed and bring her to a state of physical and emotional equilibrium. Her body was set to a position of pain and, when sex came into it, force or coercion was required for satisfaction and release.

Many people express the wish for pain or coercion as an accompaniment to sexual arousal. There is a plethora of internet sites dedicated to sex and violence. The recent survey carried out by Brett Kahr for his book *Sex and the Psyche*, in which he details his interviews with 19,000 adults, many of whom revealed cruel or sadistic fantasies as an important mental adjunct to sexual activity, tells us a troubling story of bodies which have been violated.[11] His work and the preponderance of graphically violent internet sex suggest that we

crave intense physical sensations to cut through the preoccupations and consequences of the visual and sexualised eleva-
tion of the body. The body as ordinary, and ours, eludes us. We
search for it in disturbing ways.

Once our bodies were used to make things – to build dams
and stone walls, plough fields, paint frescoes, scrub clothes,
gather the needs of daily life. Now those who work with their
bodies many hours a day are a class apart. Millions of us work
only with our fingers on keyboards. We admire the sportsperson or team for their physical skills; we may garden, walk, dance
and swim for pleasure and health, but we are exceptional if we
do not have to make an effort to 'use' our bodies. Starting with
our electric toothbrushes and power showers in the morning
and ending with our remote-control TV buttons at night,
through escalators, lifts, cars, bicycles, motorised leaf blowers,
computer technology, central heating and air conditioning,
the most mundane of physical adjustments are achieved. No
wonder public health pronouncements remind us to walk. We
insulate ourselves and provide comfort for our bodies, displac-
ing much of the labour process that, historically and organically, involved them and worked specific muscles shaping them
in ways that revealed that labour. And although we would not
necessarily wish to revisit an age of physical hardship and scar-
city, we undoubtedly face a predicament as we struggle to find
new functions and purposes for our bodies. Ironically, as we
use our bodies less, the image of muscularity for men comes
to the fore. Tracking the changes to the male doll Ken (Barbie's
friend), one sees dramatically increasing chest, neck and arm
measurements, which set up a visual injunction to keep one's
body healthy, strong and ready for display. For women that
demand for display is perceived to be constant. Even comfy
clothes convey sexy stylishness. Since for many the body is

an 'it' rather than their home, this confusion about what the body is produces 'body' alienation and hence preoccupation. The hyper-sexualisation of the body has been one attempted solution for bringing some visceral intensity back to the body – although in preparing for sex, we may so sanitise the body that it is devoid of its smells and even perspiration.[12]

Sex is so crucial for both identity and physical sensation that when it comes to the travails of the male body, which can sometimes falter, there is now a little blue pill offered to nullify erectile dysfunction or reduced libido. Targeted at middle-aged men, but moving down through the street trade to younger ages as a designer 'hard cock' drug, the Viagra–Cialis concoctions are an offering to men who, faced with the lack of an erection or the fear of not sustaining an erection, reprise something of their pre-adolescent physical states, when they didn't know how their penis might react.

The unpredictability of the penis and the need to represent it as ever hard, ever available and ever in pursuit have created a mythological magical phallus which allows us to forget how devastating the effect of the labile nature of the penis can be on men's self-experience and masculine sensibility. On a psychological note, we might designate the flaccid penis as some kind of bodily truth about the man's emotions and vulnerability. Rarely, however, do we regard this as part of the normal male experience, which mostly surely it is. Our approach to virility – in which women can feel rejected by a flaccid penis and in which men can feel alarmed – compounds the problem. The occasional loss of an erection should not be regarded as troublesome. The experience can increase intimacy as two people share something unexpected. Individual women and male partners reassure and console their men. But despite what individual couples create between them, a general view designates the unpredictable penis as a sign of inadequacy, with the consequence that worry about a lack of potency can turn the occasional 'mishap' into a persistent impotence, driving men to pills and potions.

Jerry was in his forties, sexually active with his wife (and occasionally, more excitingly, with anonymous men). He felt he had 'lost his manhood' because he could not rely on an erection during sex. He started messing up at work. He began frantically to take chemical aids, which, while helping him to relax when contemplating or having sex, then made him anxious that his erection was pharmaceutically induced rather than the real thing. He lived in fear that the truth about him had finally been exposed: he was a fraud. Like many people who come to psychoanalysis, he wanted both to confront this 'truth' and to hide from it. He feared it would dismantle him. He especially worried about the loss of the sexual self that had accompanied his sense of masculinity from his teenage years.

Initially in therapy he talked about sex. He wanted to revisit his past in the military, where he had worked until service retirement. He started with a story I'd read and heard many times but which I had never been told in therapy. The night before he first shipped out as a marine, he had followed the folkloric tradition of putting his pistol under his girlfriend and having intercourse on top of it and her. He was several generations on from the ditty 'Here is my rifle, here is my gun, this one's for fighting, this one's for fun'. But the linking of weaponry and the penis was well established in his marine company and within him. 'This is me,' he said. 'I am two things: a rifle and a gun.' He also told me, 'I am other things too, but this is what matters.'

During basic training, he and the other recruits were commanded by drill instructors to name their rifles after their girlfriends. You bond with your gun the way you bond with your 'girl' so that, in the very act of becoming a killer, you are girded by the comfort of a sexual-emotional relationship.[13]

Jerry was trained to be on high alert: available for orders and available for sex. For many of his twenty years as a professional marine, and then working in the security business, he had come to rely on his capacity to deliver, whether on the job, attending to family duties, playing sports or romancing and having sex. But he was depressed. He went through the motions, was dutiful, but felt empty inside. When his erection was no longer reliable, he told himself he was in big trouble.

In therapy, Jerry spoke about his body and what he had experienced as if he was an instructor taking us through a training manual. As he began to loosen up from the fright of talking about himself, he described his body variously as his failing tool, as numbed and cut off, or, more graphically, as a killing machine. The difficulty he had with his penis was a route into unpacking the horrors of training and war, now some years in the past but which had formed so much of his physical and psychological sense of self.

As a young African-American man growing up in the ghetto of Chicago's South Side, Jerry had needed to be tough. The marines reinforced something he already knew. His body had been built to fight and to conquer and that was how he saw sex as well. In talking, he began to find words and feelings which loosened an internal armature that had squashed vulnerabilities that had existed for him (and doubtless thousands of other recruits) before he became a marine. Confronting just how tough he had needed to be and how tough he was on himself was very painful for him. It melted down his known ways of being. He felt disarmed. At times he felt he was questioning everything he had known and done – his reactions, his emotional responses, his ideas about life. He was scared. And scared was a feeling he'd not allowed himself to experience. It was a feeling he used to whack away with bravado and shows of 'tough' behaviour. The process of therapy was paced to still his fear enough for him to realise he could experience it without running and that we could live through deconstructing the militarised body he had assumed.

The militarisation of Jerry's body had turned it into a weapon – against others and against himself. How could it be otherwise when he had fashioned it in such a regimented way? He tried to hold on to his heart through his sweetheart, Rosa Mae. She symbolised love, softness and comfort. That 'sweetheart package' was what the marines offered their men as a counterpoint to the brutality. But for Jerry, and for many other marines and soldiers, the rehumanisation hadn't quite worked. He was at war with the tender part of himself. The capacity to have loving relationships had degraded. It wasn't easy to marshal one part of oneself and not another. There was the soft and good sweetheart part and the killer part (with sexuality forming the bridge). But he couldn't sequester bits of himself off quite so neatly, particularly in the aftermath of binges of paid-for sex when he served overseas. And as he talked, he was overcome by war memories and images of the village rapes committed and recounted by some of his company. The recollection undid him. He had walled himself off from the horror. But now he cried and cried.

We explored how the taut body of Jerry as the killer would have an understandably difficult time emotionally detumescing into the tender body of the lover. The activities were mutually exclusive. To become a killer meant to become hardened. It also meant being reticent and frightened of reflecting on the emotional consequences and meanings of killing. That made a lot of sense to me. A woman is raised to nurture and to enable others to initiate. When a woman recognises the negative aspects of (s)mother love, it can be heartbreaking. She doesn't like to recognise the destructive parts of her socialisation and the behaviours and emotional consequences they cause, any more than Jerry wanted to face the damaging cost to himself of having been trained to kill. While female and male socialisation is loosening, it does not yet include a consciousness of what killing, or being ready to kill, entails. We are only a couple of generations away from raising a majority of our menfolk to kill. Masculinity has been entwined with the notion of valour and of vanquishing – sexual and military – and although we no longer require this capacity of all of our men, we have left those who kill or have killed in the name of military service with few resources to manage what ensues. When sex and violence are linked together by military training, the consequences for sexuality are often far from benign.

Most of our psychophysical maturity has precursors. We crawl before we walk, we pull ourselves up before we stand, we vocalise before we talk, we suckle before we chew. We limber up and slowly develop the muscles that will enable us to take on crucial human activities. When it comes to sexuality and the erotic, the situation is rather different. Although post-Freudian commentators have seen the breast and breastfeeding as a proto-sexual activity in which the baby's feelings of bliss were akin to post-orgasmic contentment, this equivalence is too farfetched for most people. Of course something about the sexual is present in the breastfeeding situation for some mothers with some babies. And something about the sexual is present in masturbatory form from early on. But this, unlike most other developments in children, doesn't bring forth an exclamation of 'Well done, darling.' We don't phone our friends and say, 'So exciting! Emma found her clitoris today.' We may not know what to say to a masturbating child. We try to convey something about privacy or appropriateness without curtailing their enthusiasms, but we do not often give language to the activity. Whatever we do or don't say and transmit is absorbed by our child as part of his or her sexual development. Familiarity with one's genitals is obviously somewhat different for girls and boys, because the placement of the urethra/penis combination means that boys are handling their sexual organs daily while girls' clitorises and labias often go untouched, unnamed and known only as 'down there'. Our many different attitudes towards our children's explorations, the way we represent sexuality ourselves and the physicality we bring to parenting form the local context for the child's sense of its sexual-sensual possibilities. Outside the home, peer culture, the sexo-commercialisation of childhood, the panic about sexual predators and pornography combine to represent sexuality in terms which are akin to either a sport, a purchase or an act of violence, so that the structuring of sexual impulses and sexual identity takes place in an arena of confusion, negativity and with plenty of voids.

The problem is particularly acute with girls. Many of the reasons for this lie in patriarchy's ambivalent relationship to women's sexuality, where women were vested with regulating their own and their daughter's sexuality. Sexuality, the erotic, bore a dual legacy of being for one's man and being for reproduction. Women who openly enjoyed their own sexuality for themselves were ostracised as bad, immoral or fallen. And while the pill separated sex from reproduction, opening up erotic possibilities for female sexuality in its own right, the girls on the school buses alert us to the ordinary difficulties girls and women today encounter in developing their sexuality. They may look as if they are doing it for the boys, but the boys' lack of readiness cues us into the fact that the girls are basically in search not so much of sex as of self-esteem. Their sexuality is what they use to try to get it. They are as confused as women twenty years older who also struggle with trying to find a sustainable sexuality.

Ruby was quite typical of many women I have seen over the years. Outwardly confident and in a stable relationship with a man, she had begun to lose interest in sex. Her desire deadened the longer she was with Ricardo, whom she loved and found attractive. When he was away, she wanted him. If they started to make out at the airport or in the car on the way home when she fetched him, she was passionate and full of longing. They now appeared to have their best sex under these conditions: conditions which might seem quite dangerous and rather uncomfortable. Ricardo didn't mind. He loved feeling her desire. If it occurred in these vaguely transgressive conditions, so be it. He had become hurt and confused by the diminishing of her sexual enthusiasm. She too felt confused. She'd been eager when they first got together.

It was important to Ruby that she looked good. When she looked at herself in the mirror, she saw a vibrant, stylish woman who resembled a designer more than a criminal lawyer. She was pleased. On the outside she looked sexy and elegant. She was mystified that her sexual desire could be so fragile. During the day, she imagined coming home to Ricardo and making love. She'd muse over the time they might spend in bed over the weekend. But once at home, all such thoughts either deserted her or became a source of self-reproach: what's wrong with me that I don't want to do it now that I have the opportunity?

When dating, Ruby and Ricardo had been captivated by

one another. Explorations about who they were and what they liked fuelled their passion. Two came to make one and the one seemed to enhance each of them individually. The dynamic interplay between passion, love, coming together and being apart nourished them sexually and spiritually. Their union created a lovely balance between togetherness and separateness which pleased them for several years, but as they entered their ninth year as a couple, with two small children, the sexual power evaporated.

Ruby wondered whether her desire dimmed because she couldn't put sex into what was now a matrimonial relationship. Was she too in love with her children, sensually engaged with them and just plain exhausted? Then there was her view of her parents' marriage, which seemed sexually dead to her. As a teenager and in her twenties she had been sexually active. Could it be that she had now stepped into her mother's shoes, where sexual desire had no place? Her mother had come from the generation in which sex was not considered especially pleasurable for women – or it wasn't meant to be. Ruby's mother had not conveyed that a rich sex life was part of what came with marriage. If anything, it was not quite nice and a bit of an obligation. While Ruby had been unaffected by such messages when she was single, now in a long-term relationship she found that only slightly transgressive sex appealed to her. Hence sex on the way home from the airport on a hard shoulder.

As we explored the issue further, it seemed that when Ruby became a mother she had taken up an unconscious identification with her own mother's negative feelings about her body and sexuality. This emerged only indirectly when Ruby talked about her daughter's body and her discomfort with its very ordinary chubbiness. It seemed – irrationally to

Ruby – to offend her. She felt it was too wobbly and uncoor-
dinated. Not that Clara, her daughter, felt this way herself. It
was Ruby who was disconcerted and felt that her daughter's
body was out of control. As we talked more, Ruby realised she
had always been very disciplined and contained about her
body and she thought now that this disciplining had been an
attempt to provide herself with a body border as an unconfi-
dent, rambunctious and clumsy little girl. Thinking back, she
felt she must have been confused about her body's external
contours. She wondered now what kind of holding and security her mother had been able to provide. Reining in her body
and being watchful had been Ruby's way to corset herself. In
doing so, she had become quite rigid. She could not be free to
take leave of her body and trust that it would do right by her,
because she unconsciously felt there would be no body for her
to return to.

This thought brings back Colette, with her false or adapted
body. Ruby, too, was constantly making temporary boundaries because she had no body surety inside her. Her not being
able to 'let go' sexually unless she was in a tight space, like a
car or somewhere fraught, was her grown-up version of creating a boundary while in an emergency (or a transgressive and
naughty) situation which gave her a sense of physical existence. The lack of an integrated sense of sexuality as rich, pleasing and erotic, coupled with a missing body boundary, meant
that once she had entered the conventional psychic space of
parenting, she lost the rebellious environment that her body
insecurity required. She needed to retransgress in order to feel
excitement.

Ruby's and Jerry's experiences challenge the notion of a
naturalistic body that simply knows how to be and how to have
sex. Jerry's is a male version of the more often cited girls' and

women's bodies I have been discussing. Jerry's sexualised military body is an exaggeration of a physically shaped masculinity – a masculinity which in idealised form once pertained to the majority of able-bodied men in the West but which is now largely found only in gyms, gangs and among certain skilled workers – steeplejacks, say, or those involved in construction – where brawn is honed to suit both particular physical purposes and to provide identity.

Jerry's experience joins with the behaviour of young girls on the school buses and on drunken binges and Ruby's transgressive sex to reveal how images of masculinity and femininity are shaping sexuality. In psychoanalytic terms, these sexualities function as defences against vulnerability. Being macho about 'doing' it – as those girls were – provides ballast against the not quite knowing what or why you are doing it. At the same time, the vulnerability that drives the behaviour is searching for an intimate relationship in which that very vulnerability can be accepted. Sexuality becomes the vehicle that allows bodies to meet, but their emotional and bodily frailty mean that unless they can accept vulnerability, not much beyond performance can happen. The body can touch and be touched, but it cannot be reached.

6

WHAT ARE BODIES FOR?

I have been advancing two different kinds of argument. The first is reasonably straightforward: that bodies are and always have been shaped according to the specific cultural moment. There has never been a 'natural' body: a time when bodies were untainted by cultural practices. How we move our hands as we speak, the way we walk, our table manners, our gait, our food, whether we mark babies at birth via circumcision or later with facial markings, whether we denigrate dark skin or long noses and even the diseases with which we are diagnosed (high blood pressure in the UK and US, low blood pressure in Germany): all these tell us that bodies belong to a specific time and place. It is not so long since John Howard Griffin's *Black Like Me* exposed how skin pigmentation determined the kind of lives people could live in the US. We are judged physically and our social and economic position has depended on how our bodies are seen and where we are then placed socially and economically. That people now challenge limitations of class, race and, latterly, the biological and gendered designations of male and female is welcomed. What may be less welcome is that globalism, which by its nature exposes the deep inequities of race and class throughout the world, simultaneously offers a story of belonging if one can superficially erase an economic poverty of background by expunging its physical markers and securing the right look, the right kind of body. Individuals, wherever they are from, inscribe their corporeality to express the cultural moment. The way they personally enact this through their body, their hair, their walk, their clothes and their accessories signals the way they wish to be seen and (re) designated. The postmodern myth of self-invention is broadcast and taken up across the world.

My other argument is about what is happening to bodies in our time. The story I have been telling is of our particular cultural moment in which we may well be the last generation to inhabit bodies which are familiar to us. In reproduction we are on the cusp of cell manipulation before implantation, gene modifications and different kinds of wombs being used. And after fertilisation, surgical enhancements, biological replacements, personally tailored pharmaceuticals. Meanwhile a legal and illegal trade in body parts, from hearts to stem cells and kidneys, exposes the commercial nature of our bodies today. While if the transhumanists are correct, computer chips to enhance brains will soon be on offer. In days gone by (and in many countries today outside the prosperous West), not all bodies survived birth and those that did wore out, became diseased and gave up. Today, we implant new body parts, procreate saviour siblings, replace what decays and resculpt bodies with a sense of a psychological entitlement to do so. Our embodiment today stands between a post-industrial moment and a time when bodies will be precision bio-engineered.[1]

Until recently, we've taken our bodies for granted. We've hoped that we would be blessed with good health and, especially if we are female, good looks. Those who saw their body as their temple, or became magnificent athletes or iconic beauties, were the exception. We didn't expect to be like them. Like gifted scientists, historians, writers, directors, explorers or cooks, their talents extended and enhanced the world we lived in, but we didn't expect this beauty, prowess or brainpower of ourselves.

But as I've shown, over the past thirty years the new grammar of visual culture, the notion of the consumer as empowered, the workings of the diet, pharmaceutical, food, cosmetic surgery and style industries, and the democratisation of aspiration have made us view the body we live in as a body we can, must and should perfect.[2]

The clash between the new imperative to be beautiful and the limited and limiting aesthetic of beauty we imbibe means that bodies in our time are constantly in need of attention. They have become less where we live from and more what we can personally manufacture. The news sections of our daily papers warn us of the consequences of not paying sufficient attention to our health, while in the feature sections we are exhorted to take action to keep ourselves in more than optimum shape. Remaking the body, whether through exercise, spiritual endeavour, food regimens, genetic counselling or cosmetic surgery (and one gets the sense that all options should really be pursued), is tinged with moral entreaty.

We no longer accept our bodies or even any body as a given. As the soldier's body has been replaced by air power and chemicals in warfare, and the worker's body has been replaced by highly calibrated robots in industrial production, the very notion of a body has become a product we manufacture and create. A fit body, a lithe body, a healthy body and a beautiful body have become both the ambition and the obligation of millions. The supersized, digitally enhanced images of airbrushed and Photoshopped individuals which penetrate into our public and private spaces are reshaping the way we regard bodies. This visual muzak, omnipresent in lifts and queues, projected everywhere to keep our eyes busy, makes us superaware and hyper-critical of our own bodies. This has created a cultural climate in which improving the way the body looks and functions is seen as a crucial personal responsibility. The body is both a statement and a site of empowerment.

Wherever we are, we seek belonging through our bodies. We make them conform by achieving a certain look, one that narrows yearly as the spread of globalism promotes the ideal- ised thin western female body as *the* body to possess. Men still have a few options, but these, too, are dwindling. Throughout the world, girls and women grapple with the asymmetry of the images that are projected and their own attempts to find a place and a body that they can live from. That these images are powerful is in no doubt. Brands invest heavily in market- ing. Their spending works. Where once religious iconography penetrated the consciousness of the people, brand iconogra- phy conveyed by particular kinds of bodies does that today. Because the market demands constant economic activity, we also become primed to change: to look out for and to yearn for those fleeting identity markers. It is not just the same coffee and clothes, shops and hotel chains with which world travel- lers can reassure themselves of continuity and belonging. It is via exhibiting the right kind of body.

Identity and bodies are formed with reference to our par- ticular world. Desire is formed in dialogue with that world. It is relational. The global economy and visual culture make an impression on individuals and as they make their response they feel themselves to be part of the world. What they have understood is that they need to be at the ready to trans- form their body. They embrace and anticipate change with a certain pleasure. Their desire for change expresses their active involvement with the global conversation about femininity and masculinity.

In Fiji, within three years of the advent of TV in 1995 11.9 per cent of teenage girls made themselves vomit up food as they wrestled to get their bodies to resemble those of western TV characters.[3] In Brazil, the formerly disregarded breast has lately become sexually desirable. Breast enlargement is now designated a necessary accompaniment to the plumping and lifting of the bottom and face.[4] Women there, as in China and Iran and Lithuania (and pretty much everywhere else in reach of global media), strive to get their bodies to reflect western norms of beauty as created and disseminated by visual culture. At a less dramatic level, diet, exercise and self-discipline – not for pleasure, but to produce the right kind of body – are the handmaidens to women's (and increasingly boys' and men's) daily experience all over the world as the search for identity is caught up with and entwines the struggle to have a body.

As women engage with the highly restricted visual language available to us, we can't help but participate in a kind of self-mutilation or violence. I am not setting this 'violence' against some notion of an innocent or inviolable body. This is too idealistic in a world where crimes of violence, from domestic and stranger rape, to physical assault, to clitoridectomies, affect so many women's lives across the five continents. I am speaking rather of the ordinary difficulties women encounter in the attempt to constitute a secure corporeality in the face of the persistent onslaught of images that make us hyper-critical of our own. In a reprise of Marx's aphorism that 'we enter a world not of our own making', women today confront a visual world not of their own making.

The new idea that our bodies are and should be an individual creation rather than the simple outcome of biology means that the body takes up enormous amounts of energy and becomes a source of considerable difficulty for many, many people today. In my practice, I have seen people with all kinds of difficulties: sexual problems, relationship problems, conflicts over parenting, work concerns, issues with identity, fear of intimacy, general insecurity and lack of confidence. Almost without exception, how individuals think and feel about their bodies has come to play an ever larger part in their notion of what is right or wrong. They believe that their bodies are a physical enunciation of their true state of being. This view of bodies has led me to raise some previously unasked questions about how we get a body.

So how *do* we get a body?

I have been suggesting that the body is made, not born. In an echo of both the writer Simone de Beauvoir's famous aphorism 'Women are made and not born' and the paediatrician and psychoanalyst Donald Winnicott's oft-quoted phrase 'There is no such thing as a baby; there is only a mothering pair', I hope I have shown that everything about our physical being is the outcome not of nature (although undoubtedly we feel natural and highly individual), but of the ways in which nature's body is treated by those who raise us.[5] The deaf couple who want a deaf baby are telling us about the terms in which they experience the body and the value of a language and culture of talking hands rather than aural language. The subtlety of speech, accent and style which we associate with the aural is found by them in the movement of the hands, fingers, arm and wrist. That is what they want to pass on and do: their children's physicality (inside the brain and outside through gesture) will be structured according to the demands of a language communicated by the hands. The Kayapo Indians from the equatorial rainforests in the Amazon, who bite rather than kiss when showing sexual affection, demonstrate the wide range of human physical expression and behaviours and their very varied meanings. What the Kayapo Indians do with, to and in front of their children 'naturally' makes for the 'natural' body of the Kayapo child and the 'natural' cultural body behaviours of their offspring. They too will bite when communicating sexually. It will be natural to them. As we have seen, interpersonal, parental, rearing relationships shape us from the outside and interpersonal, parental, rearing relationships shape us from the inside, creating the specific architecture of our personal brains.[6] The behaviours create particular and personal neural pathways which affect and structure our biology in ways that are more explicit than any genetic predisposition.

In this making of our bodies, the rich diversity of differently inscribed bodies is under threat. We are in one sense a long way from the bound feet of Chinese girls, but in another our armature and artifice (from Michael Jackson-type transformations to Korean girls westernising their eye shape) tell us about the intense struggle we individually employ to find the bodies that we can inhabit today. Just as globalism has seen whole human languages disappearing fortnightly, to be replaced by the world's dominant tongues, so too the cultural differences between bodies are under threat. The aesthetic preferences of traditional societies are being sidelined as the younger generation abandon the bodies they have grown up with and opt for the westernised body. There is a new uniformity from Caracas to Riyadh – which prevails under both the hijab of the devout Muslim and the wig and long skirt of the religious Jew. Western ideals of slimness, a particular shape of nose and youth are everywhere prized.

The standardised youthful body we see promoted and which we then endeavour to create individually is not a stable body. It can't be. Even if one happens to have an approximation of the idealised body, the scrutiny of women's size, shape and features, with the yearly modifications to the model, means that the girl or woman with a thin body can feel just as insecure. While slim has been a dominant motif since the 1960s recently tall has been added, as have big breasts and now the big, firm bottom. So even the slim body is precarious and, all too often, a source of anguish to the individual.

Yet, we cannot, of course, escape the body. Even as we take on imagined identities in cyberspace to make virtual connections with cyberised people, we cannot live in the material world without bodies. Ironically, it becomes the task of our cyber-identities, where one chooses who one wishes to be, to reveal the deep instability and slipperiness of embodied experience today, and yet how impossible it is to escape age, gender and ethnicity. From my own clinical practice, the variety of body difficulties I encounter – anorexia, self-harm, the wish to do away with a body part, eczema, sexual identity confusions, fear of ageing, compulsive exercising – can be seen as the individual's constant attempt to search for a reliable body and to rid herself or himself of body shame.

Bodily shame is often misascribed to a generalised anxiety looking for an outlet. We live in an age of anxiety in which choice and self-invention offer identities that are more fluid than those circumscribed by the categories of class, age, status and ethnicity that held such sway not so long ago.[7] Today we see people attempting to reject the confining binaries (upper class/working class, black/white, skilled/unskilled) on which so much of our social organisation has been built. But when it comes to the body, the binary of good body and bad body has not dissolved. Yes, categories of male/female, even black/white, once thought immutable, are contested. One can register at a university health centre in the US as 'intersexed' and choose how to describe one's ethnicity in forms sent out by local councils in the UK. But, in a curious unreflexive stance, the aesthetic judgement which pertains to slim and thin remains unchallenged by the postmodern turn. Few proclaim anything other than that fat is bad and thin is good. In the discourse about self-created identity, the body is central. It is central because it is a vehicle to assert one's place as a member of a class, a group, a sexual practice, an aspiration. It is central because it is a place of anxiety in itself.

This book has argued not only that bodies are made but that they are made in conditions in which the body of the infant may be treated in such a way that at its very core its physicality is rendered unstable and precarious. Body instability is rife. It is not only the dumping ground for emotional anxiety; it is a problem in its own right which needs addressing. Mostly we don't see the body's anxiety as bodily anxiety. We misread the anxiety, misinterpret the wish to change the body as aspirational and as psychologically motivated – the outcome of an unfortunate emotional issue, such as lack of control or, more commonly, an inability to digest upset or conflict which is then visited on the body as a somatic symptom. But body anxiety is as fundamental as emotional anxiety and we need to recognise this. It is essential, especially for therapists, if they wish to be of use to those who consult them. Although clinicians have sometimes been slow to see this, the work of contemporary artists is directing our gaze to this disturbing phenomenon.

The power of works by Antony Gormley, Richard Serra, Marc Quinn, Orlan, Ron Muerk and many others lies in the way they address the fragmentation and instability of the human form in the later twentieth and early twenty-first centuries. Gormley makes casts of his body. In doing so he directs us to see the lack of integrity that has come to pervade the human form. He enunciates a whole body among other whole bodies, in vivid contrast to advertising images and photography's tendency to represent bodies only in terms of part objects. He is drawing us into the beauty of the ordinary form, unperfected. His repetitive use of his own body is a means to shows us that we share a common bodiliness.

In *Blind Light*, part of his 2007 exhibition at London's Hayward Gallery, he invites us to physically experience a version of the disorientation that we habitually experience in relation to our own bodies. So pervasive is this disorientation we almost don't register it. By filling an enclosed space with fog and inviting us inside, he allows us to experience our physical disorientation as we lose our bearings. And for once we not only recognise our fundamental disorientation but are forced to experience it and acknowledge it. Gormley's work shows us the body as foundational and implies that if we could see it, experience it and trust ourselves, we might not need to change it incessantly.

The numerous exhibits on the body over the last few years alert us to a pervasive cultural dysmorphia. They tell us we've lost the plot where bodies are concerned. Consider *Body Worlds*, Gunther von Hagen's show of the plastinated dissected body with its veins and arteries, kidneys and spleen shown in situ. Or the *Spectacular Bodies* exhibition at the Hayward Gallery in 2000, which showed the medical representation of the body over the last several centuries. Or take Marc Quinn's historical referencing to the sculpted body, the morphing bodies of today's photography exhibits, the sculptural work of Richard Serra, which destabilises our physicality and balance. It is hard for anyone to punch above their weight when the media-generated visual industries go to work, but these individual artists can and they do. They amplify concerns, show us what we don't see and put into our sightline the dilemmas of our time.

To address these dilemmas and to restore the body as a reliable place to live from requires a challenge to our current beliefs and aspirations for our bodies. In our belief that the body is almost infinitely modifiable, we have become prey to industries and practices which frequently increase our sense of insecurity. We aren't being creative with our bodies and having fun with them. We are, rather, building bodies in the hope that we will create bodies that make us feel better about ourselves. I have suggested that the dictates of consumerism that pervade the work of the style industries, aided and abetted by the diet, food, pharmaceutical and cosmetic surgery industries, infiltrate the most crucial and basic of all relationships, that between a mother and her baby, shaping it in ways that inadvertently create body insecurity in the developing child. To transform this we need programmes for expectant and new mothers, to help them find some body peace inside themselves, as well as provide this for their babies.[8] We also need support for new parents so that they see their babies as having physical, touch and emotional hungers which need response rather than regulation by the clock. My clinical evidence is leading me to think that there is a 'critical period' for body acquisition, just as there is for language acquisition.[9] The critical period for body acquisition means that the body sense that one apprehends during that time, whether stable or unstable, sets one's corporeality, one's physical sense of self.[10] Teenagers' or adults' vulnerability to manipulating their body is driven by an underlying experience of body instability. Thus offering new parents support around bodily issues is crucial. It will be cheaper and more efficacious, and provide protection that can then work with the raft of so-called anti-obesity measures which governments are putting together as they search to find ways to manage what they see as the increasing number of alarmingly unbounded bodies.

In addressing the pressures on today's body, we would do

well to prosecute the diet industry for false advertising and for failing to meet trading standards. We need to expose the suspect practices on the part of the food and pharmaceutical industries which make food such a painful and emotionally dangerous area for many and we need to expand the range of body sizes included in visual culture and fashion design so that they become more reflective of bodies as they actually exist.

Celebrity culture has brought us an invidious version of sharing. By creating internationally recognisable iconic figures, it appears to be inclusive and democratic. In reality the visual nature of our world sucks out variety and replaces it with a vision that is narrow and limited as far as age, body type and ethnicity are concerned.[11] The sexualisation of our children's world is caught up with consumerism and a false erotic, leaving them as confused about the sexual as they are about where their bodies and their body-based needs begin and end.

As I conclude this book, I do so with a plea for us to rethink the body in such a way that we can both take it for granted and enjoy it. Our struggle is to recorporealise our bodies so that they become a place we live from rather than an aspiration always needing to be achieved. We urgently need to curtail the commercial exploitation of the body and the diminution of body variety, so that we and our children can enjoy our bodies, our appetites, our physicality and our sexuality. Our bodies should not be turned into sites of labour and commercially driven production. We need to be able to experience our diverse bodies, in the varied ways we decorate and move them, as a source of taken-for-granted pleasure and celebration. We need bodies sufficiently stable to allow us moments of bliss and adventure when, sure that they exist, we can then take leave of them.

NOTES

Introduction

1 See, for example, the story about Thomas Beatie, *New York Times*, 22 June 2008.

2 'The Rise of Bodysnarking', Hannah Seligson, *Wall Street Journal*, 16 May 2008.

3 See, for example, the studies by Desmond Morris detailed in *People Watching* (Jonathan Cape, London, 1977) and *The Naked Woman* (Jonathan Cape, London, 2004).

4 According to the *Associated Press*, 18 September 2007, a language dies every two weeks.

Chapter 1: Bodies in Our Time

1 Called Mr A in the paper by Berger and his colleagues: see B. D. Berger, J. Lehrmann, G. Larson, L. Alverno and C. Tsao, 'Non-psychotic, Non-paraphilic Self-amputation and the Internet', *Comprehensive Psychiatry*, Vol. 46, Issue 5, September–October 2005, pp. 380–83.

2 See J. C. Marshall, P. W. Halligan, G. R. Fink, D. T. Wade and R. S. J. Frackowiak, 'The Functional Anatomy of a Hysterical Paralysis', *Cognition*, Vol. 64, Issue 1, July 1997, pp. B1–8, for the reverse phenomenon.

3 Interestingly, where loss of limb is not so uncommon, as in mining accidents in southern Africa, the miners are not

so shamed about their phantoms and adopt pet names for them.

4 Ramachandran Notebook, Case 4, *Nova*, PBS TV, 23 October 2001.

5 Ramachandran has not only provided a neuroscience explanation but devised a series of procedures using mirrors that enables several phantom limb sufferers to resolve the pains in their missing but neurologically present limbs. Jonathan Miller, in discussing Ramachandran's work at the Reith Lecture 2003, made a profound point about the body–brain relationship when he suggested that we all have phantom limbs all of the time and that it is only when we lose an actual limb that we become aware of the fact that our idea and experience of a limb lives in the brain. See, for example, P. Haggard, M. Taylor-Clarke and S. Kennett, 'Tactile Perception, Cortical Representation and the Bodily Self', *Current Biology*, Vol. 13, Issue 5, 4 March 2003, pp. R170–73.

6 And we have become accustomed, especially in the UK with the writings of Jan Morris, to answering that yes, sexual reassignment has worked.

7 Interview with Aleshia Brevard by Mary Weaver in Nancy N. Chen and Helene Moglen (eds.), *Bodies in the Making: Transgressions and Transformations* (New Pacific Press, Santa Cruz, California, 2006).

8 And a few years later too, when Pete Seeger sang Malvina Reynolds's 'Little Boxes' about conformity.

9 Consider how hard-wearing blue jeans were once iconic of the industrial or construction worker and how, in the post-industrial age, the suitably torn and distressed look is worn by those across the class spectrum, the only physical effort

now involved deciding which fit better, those from Levi's, Abercrombie, Gap or Miss Sixty, etc.

10 Professor Harvey Molotch makes the point that the working-class male body of developed musculature is accompanied by kinetics of big movements, particular types of gestures (somewhat differentiated by type of job: lifting versus swinging, etc.) which were historically valued with high tolerance or even admiration for their gestural excesses. But, he says, in the service economy, such movements are not at all admired and this way of being in the world becomes an economic and social liability. It's not just a matter of strength and muscle, but the habituated kinetics linked in with them.

Chapter 2: Shaping the Body

1 Many children have phases of daydreaming that their parents are not their true parents and invent or hope for more adventurous childhood homes.

2 *How We Get a Body*, BBC Radio 4, 14 February 2003, produced by Jo Glanville, written and presented by Susie Orbach.

3 Bhutan received television only in 1999, so was protected from intense outside influences until quite recently.

4 See G. Rizzolatti, L. Fogassi and V. Gallese, 'Neurophysiological Mechanisms Underlying the Understanding and Imitation of Action', *Nature Reviews Neuroscience*, Vol. 2, September 2001, pp. 661–70. Also *Nova*, PBS TV, 25 January 2005.

5 See, for example, D. E. Glaser, J. S. Grezes, B. Calvo, R. E. Passingham and P. Haggard, 'Functional Imaging of Motor

Experience and Expertise During Action Observation', presented in Neuroscience Poster, 2003.

6 *How We Get a Body*, BBC Radio 4, 14 February 2003, produced by Jo Glanville, written and presented by Susie Orbach.

7 There is an interesting – albeit somewhat contentious – hypothesis that one difference between children diagnosed with autism and those considered socially adept is a lack in the mirror neuron system. Certainly, among the measures used to diagnose autism is a certain 'unrelatedness', a reluctance to look at another and an absence of feeling *for* another. Standing in another's body and in their mind is what makes for human relatedness.

8 See C. Trevarthen, 'Descriptive Analyses of Infant Communicative Behaviour', in H. R. Schaffer (ed.), *Studies in Mother–Infant Interaction* (Academic Press, London, 1977).

9 See H. Harlow, 'The Nature of Love', *American Psychologist*, Vol. 13, 1958, pp. 673–85. Harlow was picking up on John Bowlby's revelatory work on attachment and the significance of the maternal figure in the child's sense of security and well-being. See also Ashley Montagu, *Touching: The Human Significance of the Skin* (Columbia University Press, New York, 1971).

10 Tiffany Field's work is important here. See, for example, her *Touch Therapy* (Churchill Livingston, New York, 2000).

11 See S. Ludington, 'Energy Conservation During Skin-to-Skin Contact Between Premature Infants and Their Mothers', *Heart and Lung*, Vol. 19, Issue 5, 1990, pp. 445–51.

12 There is interesting work on peripersonal space, the perception of the body and the use of tools which may in time shed

light on this phenomenon, and I thank Ashish Ranpura for directing me to it. See A. Maravita, C. Spence and J. Driver, 'Multisensory Integration and the Body Schema: Close to Hand and Within Reach', *Current Biology*, Vol. 13, 2003, pp. R531–9. See also S. Orbach, 'What can we learn from the therapist's body', *Attachment and Human Development* Vol. 6, Issue 2, pp. 141–50.

Chapter 3: Speaking Bodies

1 This can sound mysterious, but there is a physical basis. The neurology involved is right-brain-to-right-brain communication, bypassing the language centres in the left side of the brain: see Allan Schore, *Affect Regulation and the Origins of the Self: The Neurobiology of Emotional Development* (Lawrence Erlbaum, Hillsdale, NJ, 1994).

2 Although it might be if it was felt to be a collusive venture in which therapist and patient unconsciously agree not to disturb a defensive structure. See S. Orbach, *The Impossibility of Sex* for a fuller discussion and examples of the therapist's process.

3 For a further discussion of this case, see Susie Orbach, 'Countertransference and the False Body', *Winnicott Studies*, No. 10 (Karnac Books, London, 1995).

4 See C. Gilham, J. Peto, J. Simpson, E. Roman, T. O. B. Eden, M. F. Greaves and F. E. Alexander, 'Day Care in Infancy and Risk of Childhood Acute Lymphoblastic Leukaemia: Findings from UK Case-Control Study', *British Medical Journal*, Vol. 330, 4 June 2005, pp. 1294–7.

5 Made up of Key Attachment Researchers Professor Miriam Steele and Bernadette Buhl-Nielsen, PhD candidate

Tiffany Haick, psychoanalysts Susie Orbach, Luise Eichen-baum, Carol Bloom, Jean Petrucelli and Catherine Baker-Pitts, movement psychotherapist Suzi Tortora, paediatric massage therapist Linda Garofallou, clinical psychologist Professor Lisa Rubin and graduate students Winter Halmi, Michelle Foster, Kathleen Hartwig and Esther McBirney.

6 See L. Sander, 'Thinking Differently', *Psychoanalytic Dialogues*, Vol. 12, 2002, pp. 11–42, shows how babies and mothers co-regulate if they are left to do so. See also L. Sander, 'Infant and Caretaking Environment', in E. J. Anthony (ed.), *Explorations in Child Psychiatry* (Plenum, New York and London, 1975).

7 Defence structures can sound both airy-fairy, as though they are just the technical creation of psychoanalysts to explain what they observe in the clinical situation, and inappropriately concrete, as they can simultaneously evoke images of battlements and barriers in the mind.

8 Of course, as the neuroscientist Daniel Glaser says, the brain is topological, so it isn't really accurate to describe right-brain-to-right-brain relating. It is more akin to arrondissements relating to one another, but this idea is used to demonstrate the impact of interaction.

9 See Allan Schore, *Affect Regulation and the Origins of the Self*; Mark Solms and Oliver Turnbull, *The Brain and the Inner World: An Introduction to the Neuroscience of Subjective Experience* (Karnac Books, London, 2002); Margaret Wilkinson, *Coming into Mind: The Mind–Brain Relationship* (Routledge, London and New York, 2006); Jan Panskeep, *Affective Neuroscience: The Foundations of Human and Animal Emotions* (Oxford University Press, New York, 1998).

10 See Steven Rose, *The Making of Memory: From Molecules to Mind* (Bantam Books, London, 1993); G. M. Edelman, *Second Nature: Brain Science and Human Knowledge* (Yale University Press, New Haven, Conn., 2006).

11 See Susie Orbach, *Hunger Strike* (Faber and Faber, London, 1986).

12 See Susie Orbach, *Fat is a Feminist Issue* (Paddington Press, New York and London, 1978); Carol Bloom, Andrea Gitter, Susan Gutwill, Laura Kogel and Lela Zaphiropoulos, *Eating Problems* (Basic Books, New York, 1994).

13 See Judith Butler, *Gender Trouble: Feminism and the Subversion of Identity* (Routledge, New York, 1990).

14 See Susie Orbach, 'There's No Such Thing as a Body', in Kate White (ed.), *Touch: Attachment and the Body* (Karnac Books, London, 2004).

15 Often therapists fail to give their patients the opportunity to find bodies for themselves because their personal body anxieties are so severe that sitting with two anxious, self-hating or bodyless bodies is too difficult.

Chapter 4: Bodies Real and Not So Real

1 Report on Bloomberg TV, August 2007, reporter Lisa Rapaport: Lrapaport1@bloomberg.net.

2 See Catherine Baker-Pitts, 'Symptom or Solution? The Relational Meaning of Cosmetic Surgery for Women', unpublished dissertation, New York University, 2008.

3 Particularly with the harvesting of an individual's stem cells, which, once extracted, can be grown in vitro and then the autologous tissue used for reconstruction and rejuvenation. See S. Saraf, 'Role of Stem Cells in Plastic Surgery',

Indian Journal of Plastic Surgery, Vol. 39, Issue 1, 2006, p. 110.

4 BBC 4, *Visions of the Future*, 5 November 2007.

5 See E. R. Mayhew, *The Reconstruction of Warriors* (Green-hill Books, London, 2004).

6 One wonders whether the delivery of cosmetic surgery messages on TV adds to the mesmerising appeal. TV has long been known to affect brain regions differentially, harnessing right-brain emotional experiencing. See H. E. Krugman, 'Brain Wave Measures of Media Involvement', *Journal of Advertising Reasearch*, Vol. 11, Issue 1, 1971, pp. 3–9.

7 Many doctors in the West who carry out procedures are not trained in plastic surgery and there are reports that in other regions procedures are performed by unqualified people. See *Teens and Plastic Surgery: A Literature*, Review Strategy One, June 2007.

8 Mike Testa, President of CareCredit, as quoted in Natasha Singer, 'The Democratization of Plastic Surgery', *International Herald Tribune*, 17 August 2007.

9 Argentinians of middle and upper socio-economic levels have health insurance. A middle-level plan provides for one aesthetic surgery every three years. Many thanks to Marina Fernie for providing this information.

10 The Dove Campaign for Real Beauty has tried to buck the trend by presenting untouched pictures of women over fifty which celebrate their looks, energy and experience. For my involvement with Dove, see S. Orbach, 'Fat is an Advertising Issue', *Campaign*, June 2005.

11 PBS TV, *Real Savvy Moms*, 2008.

12 In *Losing the Dead*, Lisa Appignanesi writes of going to Warsaw in the 1990s and being struck by how bare the sides

of buildings were, so accustomed was she to the western adornments of advertising posters.

13 Of course there was a shared religious iconography of Christian, Ottoman, Hindu, etc. imagery accompanying missionary activity, to unite followers, to provide a sense of belonging and to remind them of the importance of their spiritual or political leaders.

14 See U. Dimberg, M. Thunberg and K. Elmehed, 'Unconscious Facial Reactions to Emotional Facial Expressions', *Psychological Science*, Vol. 11, 2000, pp. 86–9.

15 Evidence is hard here but I am grateful to William Eccleshare, Hamish Pringle and Geoff Russell for trying to clarify the number of images seen. Edwin Ebel, Chairman of General Foods, estimated the number to be 1,518 a day for a family of four in 1962. A more recent figure is 600–625 per person per day. See 'Our Rising Ad Dosage: It's Not as Oppressive as Some Think', *Media Matters*, 15 February 2007; see also Hamish Pringle and Peter Field, *Brand Immortality* (Kogan Page, London, 2008).

16 See Lauren Collins, 'Pixel Perfect', *New Yorker*, 12 May 2008, for a fascinating account of the world of digital retouching.

17 Hence the fascination of 'ordinary' photos of the famous in magazines such as *Heat*. To see an icon represented in an unkempt fashion is a revelation but also a source of longing, for it provides a tiny dent in the polished representations with which we are more familiar.

18 Steel: Global Industry Guide, Datamonitor, 2 August 2007.

19 UK growth rate from 2008 is predicted to be 2.2 per cent, leaving the beauty industry streets ahead.

20 See Lauren Collins, 'Pixel Perfect', for the way Pascal Dangin thinks about morphing knees.

21 This figure is used extensively but it is hard to pin down what it excludes.

22 I am not implying that this is the total US spend on education but it is what the government spend is (figure from usgovernmentspend.com).

23 The calculation is as follows: a 300 million population; children constitute 31 per cent of the population, so approximately 100 million; 35 million are over sixty-five and 1.47 million are in prison, therefore 164 million are spending $100 billion.

24 A study done by Cynthia Bulik, Distinguished Professor of Eating Disorders at University of North Carolina, Chapel Hill, and Lauren Reba Harrelson for *SELF* magazine, May 2008 (and presented at the Academy of Eating Disorders International Conference in Seattle in May 2008), showed that 75 per cent of women report disordered eating behaviours or symptoms consistent with eating disorders, so three out of four have an unhealthy relationship with food or their bodies. Excluding those with actual eating disorders, 67 per cent of women are trying to lose weight; 53 per cent of dieters are already at a healthy weight and are still trying to lose weight; 39 per cent of women say concerns about what they eat or weigh interfere with their happiness; 37 per cent regularly skip meals to try to lose weight; 27 per cent would be 'extremely upset' if they gained just five pounds; 26 per cent cut out entire food groups; 16 per cent have dieted on 1,000 calories a day or fewer; 13 per cent smoke to lose weight; 12 per cent often eat when they're not hungry; 49 per cent sometimes do. Eating habits that women think are normal – such as banishing

carbohydrates, skipping meals and in some cases extreme dieting – may actually be symptoms of disordered eating.

25 See T. Mann, A. J. Tomiyama, E. Westling, A.-M. Lew, B. Samuels and J. Chatman, 'Medicare's Search for Effective Obesity Treatments: Diets are Not the Answer', *American Psychologist*, Vol. 62, Issue 3, April 2007, pp. 220–33.

26 See the extended interview with the key theorist of set point, Rudolph Leibel, in *Scientific American*, 8 August 1996.

27 I was told this by the UK manager of WeightWatchers in 1979 in the green room after a *Man Alive* debate on BBC TV. She said it with dismay, as she was concerned about how unsuccessful the company was in helping people to keep the weight off and asked for advice on how they could approach the psychology of compulsive eating. Rudolph Leibel also suggests this figure in his 1996 interview in *Scientific American* just cited.

28 See Alice Mundy, *Dispensing with the Truth: The Victims, the Drug Companies, and the Dramatic Story behind the Battle of Fen-phen* (St Martin's Press, New York, 2001).

29 But according to J. Eric Oliver in *Fat Politics: The Real Story Behind America's Obesity Epidemic* (Oxford University Press, New York, 2005), p. 29, the International Obesity Task Force is in fact funded by drug companies who are involved in the development and promotion of drugs sold to treat obesity.

30 *Observer*, 2 September 2007, quoting from *Health – Third Report*, published by the House of Commons, May 2004.

31 See Susie Orbach, *Hunger Strike* (Faber and Faber, London, 1986).

32 See Susie Orbach, *Fat is a Feminist Issue* (Paddington Press, New York and London, 1978).

33 J. Eric Oliver has a nice discussion of Quetelet in *Fat Politics*.

34 It is hard to believe that the BMI serves our health interests. The War on Obesity, as it is so often described, seems to have the added purpose of creating 'the other side of the tracks' picture of the fat, as though fat people were slightly contaminated and potentially contaminating: a class of people whose habits and practices are unwelcome and whom we should avoid.

35 See K. M. Flegel, B. I. Graubard, D. F. Williamson and M. H. Gail, 'Excess Deaths Associated with Underweight, Overweight and Obesity', *Journal of the American Medical Association*, Vol. 293, Issue 15, 20 April 2005, pp. 1861–7.

36 See, for example, Marion Nestle, *Food Politics: How the Food Industry Influences Nutrition and Health* (University of California Press, Berkeley, 2002); Tim Lang and Michael Heasman, *Battle for Minds, Mouths and Markets* (Earthscan, London, 2004); Eric Schlosser, *Fast Food Nation* (Penguin, London, 2002); Greg Critser, *Fat Land* (Allen Lane, London, 2003); Ellen Ruppel Shell, *The Hungry Gene* (Atlantic Monthly Press, New York, 2002); Felicity Lawrence, *Eat Your Heart Out* (Penguin, London, 2008).

37 See Orbach, *Fat is a Feminist Issue*.

38 Baker-Pitts (2008) makes the point that the cosmetic surgery industry too reinforces the morality underlying the notion of the body as an ongoing work in progress.

39 This relates to the argument about hyperinsulinaemia. See also Greg Crister's *Fat Land*, for his discussion of the use of corn syrup and the ways in which fructose (high fructose corn syrup) is involved in metabolic shunting.

40 See Paul Campos, *The Obesity Myth* (Gotham Books, New York, 2004); Oliver, *Fat Politics*; D. E. Alley and V. W.

Chang, 'The Changing Relationship of Obesity and Disability, 1988–2004', *Journal of the American Medical Association*, Vol. 298, Issue 17, 7 November 2007, pp. 2020–27. Also *The Investigation*, BBC Radio 4, 22 November 2007.

41 See, for example, the work of James Hughes from Trinity College, Connecticut, or Professor John Harris from Manchester University, author of *Enhancing Evolution: The Ethical Case for Making People Better* (Princeton University Press, Princeton, NJ, 2007).

42 This formulation is interesting because it would seem to directly contradict the work of neuroscientists, and specifically António Damásio, who argue that brain studies are showing that our thinking follows our feelings rather than our thinking being a super-executive who directs and controls them.

43 Why people seek to go on these shows – what prompts their wish for recognition – is of course another matter.

Chapter 5: And So to Sex

1 Many thanks to Dr Audrey Jamas for alerting me to this phenomenon.

2 Or woman or man, as the site goes up to forty plus.

3 See Michael D. Lemonick, 'Teens Before Their Time', *Time*, 22 October 2000. Many other major US research organisations have documented this phenomenon. Most recently, in 2007, the American Psychological Association issued a report citing a vast number of contributing causes to the sexualising of young girls, including music videos, magazines targeted at girls, television and advertising: see 'Report of the APA Task Force on the Sexualization of

Girls', American Psychological Association Task Force on the Sexualization of Girls, 2007.

4 In 1983 Judy Lever and Vivienne Pringle set up Blooming Marvellous, making stylish and affordable clothes for pregnant women.

5 I am grateful to Rebecca Mordant of Crazy Little Girls for this fact and the subsequent information about *Sunday Sport*'s competition too.

6 See Susie Orbach, *The Impossibility of Sex* (Allen Lane, London, 1999).

7 See E. P. Spector, *The Sexual Century* (Yale University Press, New Haven, Conn., 1999).

8 See, for example, Juliet Mitchell, *Psychoanalysis and Feminism* (Penguin, Harmondsworth, 1974); Jean Strouse (ed.), *Women and Analysis* (Grossman, New York, 1974); Luise Eichenbaum and Susie Orbach, *Outside In-Inside Out* (now published as *Understanding Women*) (Penguin, Harmondsworth, 1982); Lisa Appignanesi, *Mad, Bad and Sad* (Virago, London, 2008).

9 See S. Orbach, 'Chinks in the Merged Attachment: Generational Bequests to Contemporary Teenage Girls', *Studies in Gender and Sexuality*, Vol. 9, Issue 3, 2008.

10 Also mother–daughter related, as in the French film *The Piano Teacher*.

11 Brett Kahr is making important theoretical arguments about sexuality, the emotional and physical invasion of the integrity of the body in childhood and adult sexual fantasies: see *Sex and the Psyche* (Penguin, London, 2007).

12 Parenthetically, it is a revelation to young women that vaginal odours are not the worst thing in the world, for they have been brought up to deodorise and wax their vaginal areas back into a prepubescent appearance and smell.

13 The practice of naming one's rifle after a woman in Jerry's drill company followed a tradition of personalising weaponry of all kinds. The bombs that destroyed Hiroshima and Nagasaki towards the end of the Second World War were called Big Man and Fat Boy. In these instances the atom bombs were granted a more explicit phallic status: shooting one's wad was elided with the most explosive and destructive ways that man had designed. The spurt of semen in orgasm equals the explosive power of the smashed atom. Why, a woman's mind asks, why? Why are destruction and killing so linked with the male organ? And then, having made that connection, what is the function of naming the B-29 that dropped the A bomb, Enola Gay, after one's mother, as was done by its pilot, Colonel Tibbets?

Chapter 6: What are Bodies for?

1 See 'Life after Superbabe', *Nature*, Vol. 454, 17 July 2008, p. 253. Biologists believe that treatments using cells from skin called induced pluripotent stem cells could replace IVF and that parents would be able to choose a so-called designer baby, selecting their child based on characteristics such as hair colour, height, disease-free genes, etc.

2 This is now so well integrated within US culture that there is a book for children, *My Beautiful Mommy*, written by cosmetic surgeon Michael Salzhauer, to enable mothers to talk with their children about the beauty surgery they are having. My thanks to Nancy Etcoff of Harvard for bringing this to my attention.

3 A. E. Becker, R. A. Burwell, D. B. Herzog, P. Hamburg and S. E. Gilman, 'Eating Behaviours and Attitudes Following

Prolonged Exposure to Television among Ethnic Fijian Adolescent Girls', *British Journal of Psychiatry*, Vol. 180, June 2002, pp. 509–14.

4 It is the third most popular cosmetic procedure after lipoplasty and botox.

5 Daniel Glaser points out that most of what people ascribe to the body and what the body learns is in essence a brain activity. We experience it in the body and we ascribe attributes to the body – a good hand, a good eye, muscle memory and so on – but this activity is occurring in the brain.

6 Felicity Lawrence quotes Joseph Hibbeln in her excellent book *Eat Your Heart Out* (Penguin, London, 2008) on the way in which prenatal nourishment affects the brain's architecture: see pp. 204–5.

7 See Sara Dunant, *The Age of Anxiety* (Virago, London, 2000); Renata Salecl, *On Anxiety* (Routledge, London, 2004).

8 See www.any-body.org for a program for midwives and health visitor training to increase awareness of body difficulties in pregnant women and to provide them with interventions that will target both mothers and their babies.

9 We accept now that psychological development is largely set by early childhood experience. In addition, of course, emotional misrecognition from developmental deficits can produce body dysmorphia: see U. Buhlmann, R. J. McNally, N. L. Etcoff, B. Tuschen-Caffier and S. Wilhelm, 'Emotion Recognition Deficits in Body Dysmorphic Disorder', *Journal of Psychiatric Research*, Vol. 38, Issue 2, March–April 2004, pp. 201–6.

10 This is part of the work of the Body Attachment Group.

11 The campaign to bring more black and minority models to the catwalk and covers of fashion magazines attests to this.

Anderson, F. S. (ed.), *Bodies in Treatment* (The Analytic
Press, Hillsdale, NJ, 2008)

Angier, N., Woman: An Intimate Geography (Virago,
London 1999)

Appignanesi, L., *Mad, Bad and Sad* (Virago, London, 2008)
— *Losing the Dead* (Chatto & Windus, London 1999)

Aron, L., and Sommer Anderson, F., *Relational Perspectives
on the Body* (The Analytic Press, Hillsdale, NJ, 1998)

Baker-Pitts, C., 'Sympton or Solution? The Relational
Meaning of Cosmetic Surgery for Women' (unpublished
dissertation, New York University, 2008)

Barry, B., *Fashioning Reality* (Key Porter Books, Toronto,
2007)

Becker, A., *The Body, Self and Society: The View from Fiji*
(University of Pennsylvania Press, Philadelphia, 1995)

Berg, F. M., *Children and Teens Afraid to Eat* (Healthy Weight
Network, Hettinger, ND 1997)

Berger, B. D., Lehrmann, G., Larson, G., Alverno, L. and
Tsao, C., 'Non-psychotic, Non-paraphilic Self-amputation
and the Internet', *Comprehensive Psychiatry*, Vol. 46, Issue
5, 2005, pp. 380–83

Bick, E., 'Further Considerations on the Functions of
the Skin in Early Object Relations', *British Journal of
Psychotherapy*, Vol. 2, Issue 4, 1986, pp. 292–9

Bloom, C., Gitter, A., Gutwill, S., Kogel, L., and
Zaphiropoulos, L., *Eating Problems* (Basic Books, New
York, 1994)

Bowlby, J., *The Making and Breaking of Affectional Bonds* (Tavistock, London, 1976–8)

Brunet, O., and Lezine, I., *I Primi Anni del Bambino* (Armando, Rome, 1966)

Butler, J., *Gender Trouble: Feminism and the Subversion of Identity* (Routledge, New York, 1990)

Campos, P., *The Obesity Myth* (Gotham Books, New York, 2004)

Carroll, R., www.thinkbody.co.uk

Chen, N. N., and Moglen, H. (eds.), *Bodies in the Making: Transgressions and Transformations* (New Pacific Press, Santa Cruz, California, 2006)

Collins, L., 'Pixel Perfect', New Yorker, 12 May 2008

Critser, G., *Fat Land* (Allen Lane, London, 2003)

Damásio, A., *The Feeling of What Happens* (William Heinemann, London, 1999)

Davis, K., *Reshaping the Female Body: The Dilemma of Plastic Surgery* (Routledge, London and New York, 1995)

Dickenson, D., *Body Shopping* (Oneworld Publications, Oxford, 2008)

Dimberg, U., Thunberg, M. and Elmehed, K., 'Unconscious Facial Reactions to Emotional Facial Expressions', *Psychological Science*, Vol. 11, 2000, pp. 86–9

Dunant, S., *The Age of Anxiety* (Virago, London, 2000)

Edelman, G. M., *Second Nature: Brain Science and Human Knowledge* (Yale University Press, New Haven, Conn., 2006)

Eichenbaum, L., and Orbach, S., *Outside In-Inside Out* (Penguin, Harmondsworth, 1982)

Elliot, C., *Better Than Well: American Medicine Meets the American Dream* (W. W. Norton, New York, 2003)

— 'A New Way to be Mad', *Atlantic Monthly*, Vol. 283, Issue 6, December 2000, pp. 72–84

Field, N., 'Listening with the Body', *British Journal of Psychotherapy*, Vol. 5, Issue 4, 1989, pp. 512–22

Field, T., *Touch Therapy* (Churchill Livingston, New York, 2000)

Flegel, K. M., Graubard, B. I., Williamson, D. F. and Gail, M. H., 'Excess Deaths Associated with Underweight, Overweight and Obesity', *Journal of the American Medical Association*, Vol. 293, Issue 15, 2005, pp. 1861–7

Fonagy, P., 'Transgenerational Consistencies of Attachment: A New Theory', paper to the Developmental and Psychoanalytic Discussion Group, American Psychoanalytic Association Meeting, Washington, DC, 13 May 1999

Fonagy, P., Steele, M., Steele, H., Leigh, T., Kennedy, R., Mattoon, G., and Target, M., 'The Predictive Validity of Mary Main's Adult Attachment Interview: A Psychoanalytic and Developmental Perspective on the Transgenerational Transmission of Attachment and Borderline States', in S. Goldberg, R. Muir and J. Kerr (eds.), *Attachment Theory: Social, Developmental and Clinical Perspectives* (The Analytic Press, Hillsdale, NJ, 1995, pp. 233–78)

Formaini, H., 'Some Ideas about the Father's Body in Psychoanalytic Thought', in *Landmarks*, papers by Jungian Analysts from Australia and New Zealand, 2002

Foucault, M., *The History of Sexuality*, Vol. 1, *An Introduction* (Allen Lane, London, 1978)

Gerhardt, S., *Why Love Matters: How Affection Shapes a Baby's Brain* (Brunner-Routledge, New York, 2004)

Gilman, S. L., *Making the Body Beautiful: A Cultural History of Aesthetic Surgery* (Princeton University Press, Princeton, NJ, 1999)

Gitau, R., Cameron, A., Fisk, N. M., and Glover, V., 'Fetal Exposure to Maternal Cortisol', *Lancet,* **Vol.** 352, 1998, pp. 707–8

Goldblatt, P. B., Moore, M. E., and Stunkard, A. J., 'Social Factors in Obesity', *Journal of the American Medical Association*, Vol. 192, 1965, pp. 1039–44

Grosz, E., *Volatile Bodies: Toward a Corporeal Feminism* (Indiana University Press, Bloomington, 1994)

Harlow, H. F., 'The Nature of Love', *American Psychologist,* Vol. 13, 1958, pp. 673–85

Harris, J., *Enhancing Evolution: The Ethical Case for Making People Better* (Princeton University Press, Princeton, NJ, 2007)

Kahr, B., *Sex and the Psyche* (Penguin, London, 2007)

Kaplan-Solms, K., and Solms, M., *Clinical Studies in Neuro-Psychoanalysis* (Karnac Books, London, 2000)

Kolata, G., *Rethinking Thin* (Picador, New York, 2008)

Lane, H., *The Wild Boy of Aveyron: A History of the Education of Retarded, Deaf and Hearing Children* (Harvard University Press, Cambridge, Mass., 1976)

— *The Mask of Benevolence Disabling the Deaf Community* (Knopf, New York, 1992)

Lang, T., and Heasman, M., *Battle for Minds, Mouths and Markets* (Earthscan, London, 2004)

Lawrence, F., *Eat Your Heart Out* (Penguin, London, 2008)

Leader, D. and Corfield, D., *Why Do People Get Ill?* (Hamish Hamilton, London 2007)

McDougall, J., *Theatres of the Mind: Illusion and Truth on the Psychoanalytic Stage* (Free Association Books, London, 1986)

— *Theatres of the Body* (Free Association Books, London, 1989)

Mahler, M., Bergman, A., and Pines, F., *The Psychological Birth of the Human Infant* (Basic Books, New York, 1975)

Mann, T., Tomiyama, J., Westling, E., Lew, A. -M., Samuels, B. and Chatman, J., 'Medicare's Search for Effective Obesity Treatments: Diets are Not the Answer', *American Psychologist*, Vol. 62, Issue 3, 2007, pp. 220–33

Martin, C. E. *Perfect Girls, Starving Daughters* (Free Press, New York 2007)

Marshall, J. C., Halligan, P. W., Fink, G. R., Wade, D. T. and Frackowiak, R. S. J., 'The Functional Anatomy of a Hysterical Paralysis', *Cognition*, Vol. 64, Issue 1, 1997, pp. B1–8

Mayhew, E. R., *The Reconstruction of Warriors* (Greenhill Books, London 2004)

Merleau-Ponty, M., *The Phenomenology of Perception* (Routledge & Kegan Paul, London, and Humanities Press, New York, 1962)

Miller, N. M., Fisk, N. M., Modi, N., and Glover, V., 'Stress Responses at Birth: Determinants of Cord Arterial Cortisol and Links with Cortisol Response in Infancy', *Bjog*, Vol. 112, Issue 7, 2005, pp. 921–6

Mitchell, J., *Psychoanalysis and Feminism* (Penguin, Harmondsworth, 1974)

Montagu, A., *Touching: The Human Significance of the Skin* (Columbia University Press, New York, 1971)

Mundy, Alice, *Dispensing with the Truth: The Victims, the Drug Companies, and the Dramatic Story behind the Battle of Fen-phen* (St Martin's Press, New York, 2001)

Namir, S., 'Embodiments and Disembodiments: The Relation of Body Modifications to Two Psychoanalytic Treatments', *Psychoanalysis, Culture and Society*, Vol. 11, Issue 2, 2006, pp. 217–23

Nestle, M., *Food Politics: How the Food Industry Influences Nutrition and Health* (University of California Press, Berkeley, 2002)

Oliver, J. E., *Fat Politics: The Real Story Behind America's Obesity Epidemic* (Oxford University Press, New York, 2005)

Orbach, S., *Hunger Strike* (Faber and Faber, London, 1986)

— *The Impossibility of Sex* (Allen Lane, London, 1999)

— 'Countertransference and the False Body', *Winnicott Studies*, No. 10 (Karnac Books, London, 1995)

— 'Working with the False Body', in A. Erskine and D. Judd (eds.), *The Imaginative Body* (Whurr, London, 1993)

— 'There's No Such Thing as a Body', in K. White (ed.), *Touch: Attachment and the Body* (Karnac Books, London, 2004)

— 'In Dialogue with Stephen Mitchell', *British Journal of Psychotherapy*, Vol. 15, Issue 2, 1998, pp. 194–200

— 'Chinks in the Merged Attachment: Generational — to Contemporary Teenage Girls', *Studies in Gender and Sexuality*, Vol. 9, Issue 3, 2008

Panskeep, J., *Affective Neuroscience: The Foundations of Human and Animal Emotions* (Oxford University Press, New York, 1998)

Pines, D., *A Woman's Unconscious Use of Her Body* (Virago, London, 1993)

Porter, R., *Flesh in the Age of Reason* (Penguin, London, 1993)

Pringle, H. and Field, P., *Brand Immorality* (Kogan Page, London, 2008)

Racker, H., *Transference and Countertransference* (International Universities Press, New York, 1968)

Ramachandran, V. S., 'Phantom Limbs, Neglect Syndromes, Repressed Memories, and Freudian Psychology', *International Review of Neurobiology*, Vol. 37, 1994, pp. 291–333

Rose, S., *The Making of Memory: From Molecules to Mind* (Bantam Books, London, 1993)

Sacks, O., *An Anthropologist on Mars* (Knopf, New York, 1995)

Salecl, R., *On Anxiety* (Routledge, London, 2004)

Samuels, A., *The Plural Psyche: Personality, Morality and the Father* (Routledge, London and New York, 1989)

Sander, L., 'Infant and Caretaking Environment', in E. J. Anthony (ed.), *Explorations in Child Psychiatry* (Plenum, New York and London, 1975)

— 'Thinking Differently', *Psychoanalytic Dialogues*, Vol. 12, 2002, pp. 11–42

Schlosser, E., *Fast Food Nation* (Penguin, London, 2002)

Schore, A., *Affect Regulation and the Origins of the Self: The Neurobiology of Emotional Development* (Lawrence Erlbaum, Hillsdale, NJ, 1994)

Shell, E. R., *The Hungry Gene* (Atlantic Monthly Press, New York, 2002)

Solms, M., and Turnbull, O., *The Brain and the Inner World: An Introduction to the Neuroscience of Subjective Experience* (Karnac Books, London, 2002)

Spector, E. P., *The Sexual Century* (Yale University Press, New Haven, Conn., 1999)

Spitz, R. A., 'Hospitalism: An Inquiry into the Genesis of Psychiatric Conditions in Early Childhood', *The Psychoanalytic Study of the Child*, Vol. 1 (Yale University Press, New Haven, 1945)

— 'Hospitalism: A Follow-up Report on Investigation Described in Vol. 1, 1945', *The Psychoanalytic Study of the Child*, Vol. 2 (Yale University Press, New Haven, 1946)

Stolorow, R. D., and Atwood, G. E., *Contexts of Being: The Intersubjective Foundations of Psychological Life* (The Analytic Press, Hillsdale, NJ, 1992)

Strouse, J. (ed.), *Women and Analysis* (Grossman, New York, 1974)

Taylor, G., 'Somatization and Conversion: Distinct or Overlapping Constructs?', *Journal of the American Academy of Psychoanalysis and Dynamic Psychiatry*, Vol. 31, 2003, pp. 487–508

Theweleit, K., *Male Bodies* (Polity Press, Cambridge, 1989)

Totton, N., *The Water in the Glass: Body and Mind in Psychoanalysis* (Rebus Press, London, 1998)

Trevarthen, C., 'Descriptive Analyses of Infant Communicative Behaviour', in H. R. Schaffer (ed.), *Studies in Mother–Infant Interaction* (Academic Press, London, 1977)

Wilkinson, M., *Coming into Mind: The Mind–Brain Relationship* (Routledge, London and New York, 2006)

Winnicott, D. W., 'Mind in Its Relation to the Psyche-soma', in *Through Paediatrics to Psycho-analysis* (Tavistock, London, 1958)

— 'The Capacity to Be Alone', *International Journal of Psychoanalysis*, Vol. 39, 1958, pp. 416–20

ACKNOWLEDGEMENTS

Thank you to Lisa Appignanesi for thoughtful, intelligent and patient editing. To Andrew Franklin, Frances Coady, Lesley Levene, Ruth Killick, Penny Daniel and the production staffs at Profile and Picador for their enthusiasm and professional skills. To Blake Morrison and Joseph Schwartz for reading an early version. To Natasha Fairweather, Ben Barry, Jo Glanville, Luise Eichenbaum, Carol Bloom, Emma de Sausmarez, Dan Glaser, Barbara Krebs, Catherine Baker-Pitts, Nancy Etcoff, Eva Hoffman and the members of two groups – AnyBody and the Body Attachment Group at The New School – for really useful discussions and input. To the many people I have worked with as a therapist over the years as I have endeavoured to understand bodies today. And to my dear and wondrous friends and family, thank you.

London
October 2008

INDEX

A

amputations, 13, 15–19, 21–3
Andrew: desire for
    amputation of legs,
    15–19, 21–3, 35, 54, 75
Anne (foster mother), 48–50
anorectics, 99
appetite, 99–100
Argentina: cosmetic surgery,
    85–6
athletes, 79–80
attunement (between
    mother and baby),
    59–60, 64, 67
avatars (computer
    personalities), 77–8,
    80–81
Aveyron *see* Victor (wild
    boy of Aveyron)

B

babies
    brain development,
      64–5
    crying, 62

    handling and
      engagement with, 8,
      36–41, 57–60, 63–4
    and low maternal
      weight, 104
    rhythms, 62–3, 65
    sense of self, 63, 66–7
Baker-Pitts, Catherine, 83,
    86
beauty: democratisation of,
    2–4, 12
beauty industry, 90–93
Beauvoir, Simone de, 139
Beebe, Beatrice, 36
Bell, Tony, 27–30, 33
Berger, Dr Bert, 15–16, 19, 23
Berger, John, 87
Bhutan, 147n3
Blind Light (Gormley
    exhibition, 2007), 143
bodies
    anxieties over, 141–2
    in art, 110, 142–3
    capacity to change, 23–5,
      87–92, 104, 135–6